Days of our Lives

A Tour Through Salem

Days of our Lives

A Tour Through Salem

Lorraine Zenka

A DUTTON BOOK

DUTTON
Published by the Penguin Group
Penguin Putnam Inc., 375 Hudson Street, New York, New York 10014, U.S.A.
Penguin Books Ltd, 27 Wrights Lane, London W8 5TZ, England
Penguin Books Australia Ltd, Ringwood, Victoria, Australia
Penguin Books Canada Ltd, 10 Alcorn Avenue, Toronto, Ontario, Canada M4V 3B2
Penguin Books (N.Z.) Ltd, 182–190 Wairau Road, Auckland 10, New Zealand

Penguin Books Ltd, Registered Offices: Harmondsworth, Middlesex, England

First published by Dutton, a member of Penguin Putnam Inc.

First Printing, May, 1999
10   9   8   7   6   5   4   3   2   1

LIBRARY OF CONGRESS CATALOGING-IN-PUBLICATION DATA
Zenka, Lorraine.
    Days of our lives: a tour through Salem/Lorraine Zenka.
       p. cm.
    ISBN 0-525-94302-1 (alk. paper)
    1. Days of our lives (Television program)   I. Title.
PN1992.77.D38Z457 1999
791.43′72—dc21   98-47654
                                                                         CIP
Printed in the United States of America
Designed by Stanley S. Drate/Folio Graphics Co., Inc.
Set in Stone Serif

*This book is dedicated
to devoted*
Days of our Lives
fans

Acknowledgments

The author wishes to thank the many people who contributed their time, energy, talents, and support to this project.

At the top of the list is executive producer of *Days of our Lives,* Ken Corday, for his devotion to the show and its viewers, and for taking the time to contribute to this book. And to William Bell for his enormous contribution to creating a Salem that has endured for more than three decades. Within the Corday Productions office, senior vice president, Greg Meng, and executive vice president, Gary Fogel, for their expertise and involvement.

Heartfelt thanks to Chip Dox, whose vision captured Salem architecture and geography in the skillful rendering of the Salem map and selection of exteriors; and whose kind spirit is always an inspiration. And special thanks to graphic artists Jennifer Buerklander who executed the extended floorplans and John Wiley who rendered the exteriors of Salem homes, for their skills, eye for detail, and patience.

Production designer Dan Olexeiwicz, art director Tom Early, costume designer Richard Bloore, head prop master Tom Trout, head makeup artist Gail Hopkins; *Days'* publicist David Sperber and NBC network publicist Michael Feeney for their specific expertise, dedication to the show, and contributions to this project. Likewise, music director Amy Burkhardt and viewer Patty Yocum who savor the musical moments that enhance Salem lives.

Photographer John Paschal and his staff, Aaron Montgomery, Ruby Montgomery, and Griffin Meyer for their special efforts. Kathy Hutchins for her photo contributions and support. The Web site master and diligent fan, Dustin Cushman, for his research assistance; and all of *Days'* production staff, cast, and crew for always making me feel welcome at the set.

My editor Joe Pittman for his kindness, faith, and patience. His team, which includes copy editor Sarah Haviland and book designer, Stanley S. Drate of Folio Graphics Co. Inc.

My patient family and friends who put up with my absence. And especially Robert Waldron for his patient ear, words of support, and his sense of humor.

Contents

Foreword by Executive Producer Ken Corday   ix

Preface   xi

Part One: Getting Around Salem   1

    A Map of Salem   3

Part Two: The Homes of Salem   7

    Horton Home   9

    Horton Cabin on Smith Island   18

    Fancy Face, Bo Brady's Boat   21

    The Brady Home and Pub   24

    John Black's Loft   29

    Marlena's Penthouse   34

    The Blake House   40

    The Apartment House   44

    The Carver House   54

    The Kiriakis Mansion   58

    The Deveraux House   68

    The DiMera Mansion   79

    The Alamain Mansion   89

    Roman and Marlena's House   93

    Mickey and Maggie Horton's House   95

    Salem Newcomers   96

Part Three: Salem Business District   101

    Shopping and Other Businesses   103

Spas and Gyms   110

Banks   112

The Docks   112

Media   114

Law Enforcement   120

Salem University Medical Center   126

Part Four: Salem Hot Spots   133

Hotels, Restaurants, Bars, and Clubs   135

Part Five: Beyond Salem   153

Aremid   155

The Paris Masquerade   162

The Roman Holiday   167

Hopping to Los Angeles   170

New Orleans   173

The Jungle Adventure   177

Romantic and Dangerous Getaways   179

Part Six: Salem Lifestyle   189

Churches and Parks   191

Salem's Most Memorable Weddings   198

Cast List and Credits   220

Long Crawl Credits   222

Photography and Art Credits   224

Ken Corday    Bill Bell

Foreword

O f all the many gifted and talented people who have given their time in helping to make *Days of our Lives* the success that it has been over the last thirty-two years, one person in particular must be recognized for his pioneering efforts in helping to establish the legacy that is *Days of our Lives*. That man is Mr. William J. Bell.

It is a little known fact that in the first year of *Days of our Lives,* with the death of my father, Ted Corday, and the extra pressure endured by my mother, Betty Corday, and Executive Producer, Wes Kenney, a shared vision was needed that would clarify the written direction and character of this infant show. Mr. William Bell had that vision and was the voice.

Bill took the show from the mid-sixties to the early seventies and helped lay the foundation for the creation of one of the top-rated soap operas in daytime history. I remember my mother clearly stating that had it not been for Bill Bell's talent in writing the show in its infancy, there probably would not be a *Days of our Lives* today.

Therefore, it is with humble esteem and eternal gratitude that all of us at *Days of our Lives* thank Mr. Bell for his pioneering efforts and brilliance in finding a new audience and charting new and exciting territories on *Days of our Lives* and in day-time drama in general.

Thank you, Bill, for all those many grains of sand that have passed through the hourglass and for all of the "days of our lives." May you be "young and restless" forever.

KEN CORDAY
Executive Producer
Days of our Lives

Preface

A Tour Through Salem takes us on a walk along the streets of the city to see the homes and establishments so familiar to residents but rarely visited by the viewer in depth. Just as we are flooded with memories as we walk through our own hometown, *A Tour Through Salem* provides sights that stir our hearts, with every stop along the way a reminder. It's not a history, but a scrapbook of moments in time. The happenings, the emotions of those moments, become vivid with the colors we bring to them through our own perspective.

Executive Producer Ken Corday points out that the idea for *Days of our Lives* came from soap pioneer Irna Phillips, with his parents, Ted and Betty Corday, and soon after it launched, William Bell.

"Irna continued to write *Another World,*" says Ken. "And my father died nine months after *Days* first aired in November, 1965. Then it was my mother and a first-time headwriter at the time, Bill Bell, who took it and ran with it in 1966."

Back then just as today, people who worked in large metropolitan cities often longed for a more gentle, small-town atmosphere; Salem in its early years was simply a small town with a rural, midwest geography. Doing a soap opera outside an urban environment with its tall buildings reflected that desire to enjoy life at a different pace. Over the years, as more people were attracted to its quiet charm and traditional values, Salem has grown in personality and architecture.

"Perhaps the first person who really created a geography for Salem was Pat Faulken Smith, who was headwriter in the early eighties," says Ken Corday. "She saw Salem on a river with an active waterfront area with some warehouses and homes, the Brady Fish Market, and several restaurants. She introduced Stefano DiMera and his house in an upscale neighborhood."

Although things change a bit more slowly in Salem than in other growing cities, Ken points out that "there's an amazing amount of construction going on around the NBC studios lot. There could be taller buildings around Salem Place in the next few years. But don't look for anything like high-tech people movers. Salem will maintain its charm. There was talk of a lighthouse for Bo, which sounds very romantic, but Salem, so far, has not been on a headland." More than anything else, "it's story that writes the location," he emphasizes.

For Ken, his personal walking tour of Salem would always begin right in Tom and Alice's living room. Salem Place would likely be the next stop "because there is so much to do there, and you never know who you will run into there. And the Brady Pub, of course. Then, the DiMera Mansion and Marlena's penthouse, to name a few. My memory lane is made up of a lot of public places like The Cheatin'

Heart, Doug's Place, The Salem Club, and Shenanigans. And the parks. There's a lot of greenery in town."

When Ken recalls nostalgic memories, he recalls that Roman used to mow Tom and Alice's front lawn. While growing up, Carrie Brady and Mike Horton rode their bicycles in the neighborhood and Bo and Hope, as adolescents, were always at odds over her "white picket fence" lifestyle versus his rogue-like motorcycle-driven middle-class haunts.

As we stroll through Salem, certain sights will bring to mind special memories. Savor them, and add your own.

LORRAINE ZENKA

Days of our Lives

A Tour Through Salem

Part One

Getting Around Salem

A Map of Salem

Welcome to Salem, our town . . .

North, south, east, or west. As we enter from any direction Salem streets and sites offer up memories at every turn. This is our town where we have shared hopes, dreams, life, and death.

Down shopping districts, riverfront walks, sports fields, the university and the hospital, residential streets where famous—and infamous—families live, and the airport, from which Salem residents leave and return, all pulse with the energy of the generations we know and love.

The community grows and changes over the years. Buildings come and go, streets are added, boulevards widened, new houses spring up, and old ones are renovated. Every day, the heart of Salem beats steadily. Follow the streets, visit the homes and favorite places. Find your special place. Feel the rhythm of joy and sorrow and love. Enjoy all the days of our lives!

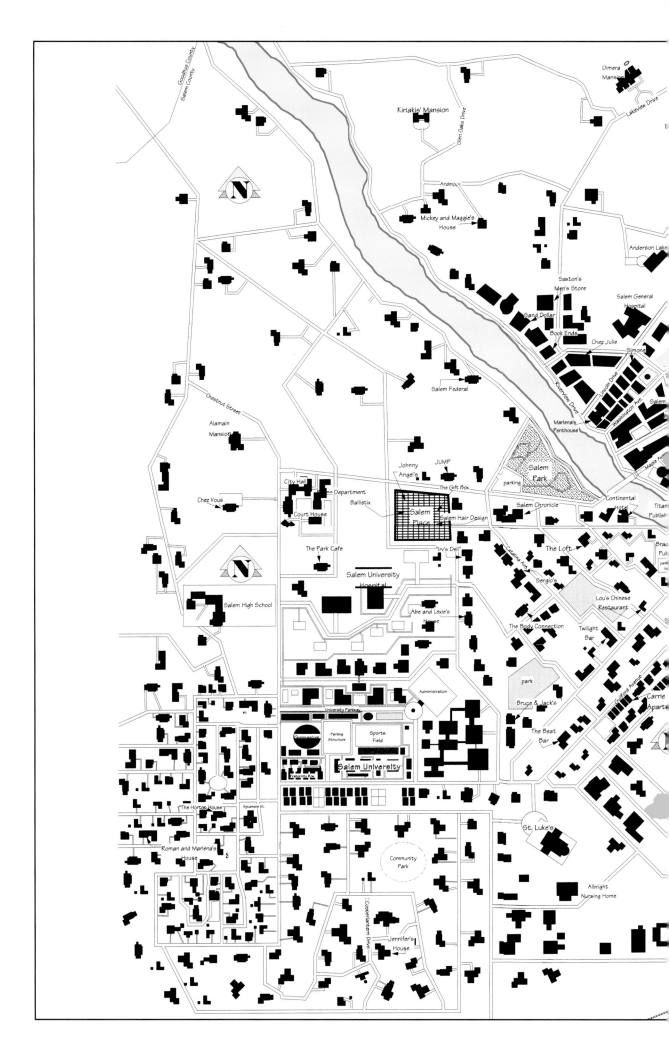

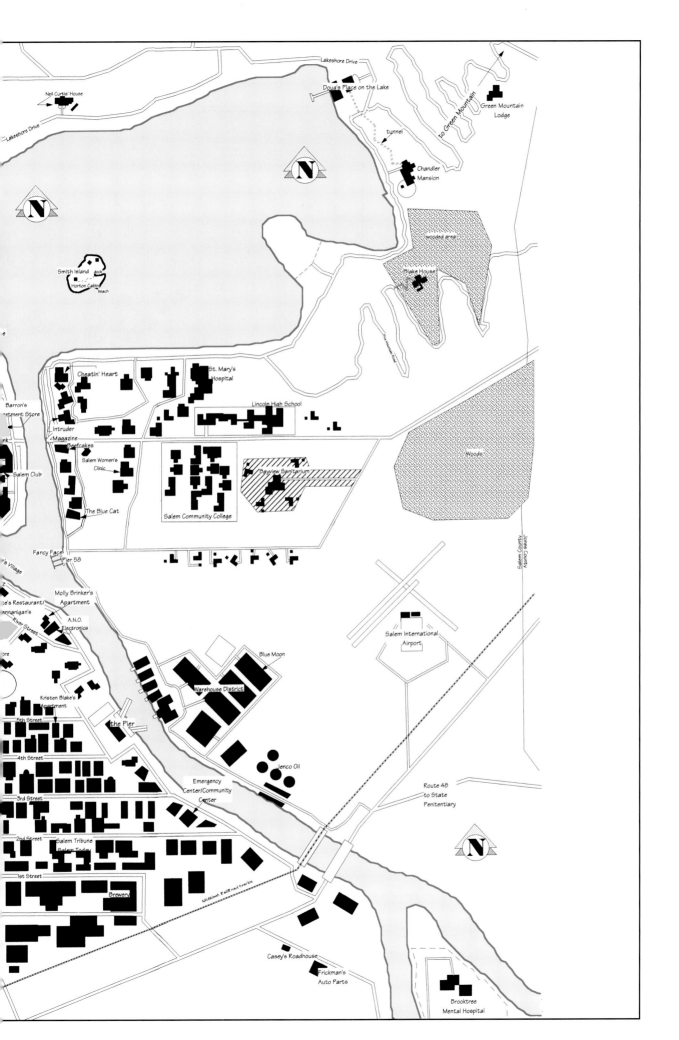

Lakeshore Drive

Neil Curtis' House

Lakeshore Drive

Doug's Place on the Lake

to Green Mountain

Green Mountain Lodge

tunnel

Chandler Mansion

wooded area

Blake House

Pine Mountain Road

Smith Island   dock
Horton Cabin
beach

Woods

Cheatin' Heart

St. Mary's Hospital

Barron's
Department Store

Lincoln High School

Intruder Magazine

Beefcakes

Salem Women's Clinic

Salem Club

Bayview Sanitarium

Salem County

Jones County

The Blue Cat

Salem Community College

Fancy Face
Pier 58

's Village

Molly Brinker's Apartment

e's Restaurant/
annanigan's

River Street

A.N.O. Electronics

Blue Moon

Salem International Airport

Kristen Blake's Apartment

5th Street

Warehouse District

the Pier

4th Street

Jenco Oil

Route 48
to State
Penitentiary

3rd Street

Emergency Center/Community Center

2nd Street

Salem Tribune
Salem Today

1st Street

Brewery

Midwest Railroad tracks

Casey's Roadhouse

Frickman's Auto Parts

Brooktree Mental Hospital

Part Two

The Homes of Salem

Horton Home

545 SYCAMORE STREET

This Georgian-style house was built a decade before Tom and Alice Horton wed and moved into it in 1930. The Horton house is in an upper-middle-class neighborhood and stands on about a quarter acre of land. It remains close to its original design. It is, for the most part, decorated with traditional Georgian-style furniture that was popular among women decorating their homes in the forties. In the fifties, there were a few things added, like a white chenile bedspread that was then popular. There are Asian accents here and there.

Alice is crazy for gardening, and especially for yellow roses. It's not unusual to see roses cut from her garden throughout the house during the appropriate season.

The living room has not changed very much over the years. Alice is very happy with her life and the sense of stability her home has provided. She likes the memories of its many private corners, like Tom's favorite tapestry-covered armchair that still stands sentry near the fireplace.

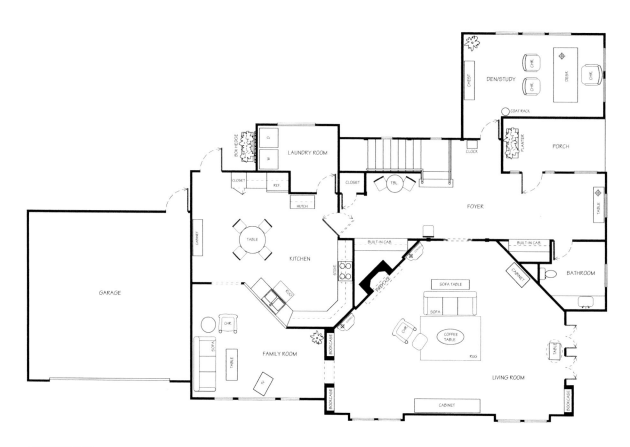

HORTON HOUSE
MAIN LEVEL

HORTON HOUSE
SECOND LEVEL

No matter what may be going on at the time, or what has occurred throughout the year, the Horton Christmas tree is decorated with special ornaments, balls with family members' names handpainted on them. The event has become a heartfelt rite of the season, a cherished time to remember and appreciate loved ones.

Of course, family patriarch Tom comes to the minds of everyone gathered and especially to Alice. The couple met while in high school and married shortly after Alice graduated—a year after Tom. After passing up a promising baseball career, Tom became a home-town doctor like his father before him. Tom and Alice shared rich memories as they raised their five children, assorted grandchildren, and great-grandchildren who came into their lives. As the Chief of Staff of the Salem University Medical Center, Tom was a pillar of the community and was loved by Salem residents who often came to him for advice and favors. Since his death, Alice has been a courageous widow, still very involved with family and community. But the loss of her life mate is always most clearly poignant as she hangs the annual tree ornament with Tom's name upon it.

In Alice's very practical and comfortable kitchen, it's common to find people talking over coffee at a wood farmhouse table. She has her family fine bone china in a hutch in the corner. The china is mostly forest green with white trim. She likes to have her coffee in a cup from that collection. The green wallpaper is complemented with copper cookware, molds, and other items. There is no microwave. But there are fresh-looking ceramics, which provide a current look, and some flowering plants. The kitchen contains a lot of what was considered Early American by 1950s standards, but the appliances (refrigerator, stove) have been updated periodically.

Alice Horton lives alone but has a constant stream of family and friends coming by to visit. She's also still active with the volunteers at the hospital.

Alice is surrounded by souvenirs gathered over decades of raising her loving family. The home she shared with her late husband, Tom Horton, brings her constant comfort.

Both Alice and Tom liked to garden and entertain family and friends in their backyard. There are white wrought-iron patio sets with a well-used barbecue in the yard. The two-car garage is kept very neat and orderly with everything in its place.

Sadly and suddenly, Tom Horton died in his sleep and was found by Alice on June 6, 1994. Alice called their son Mickey and his wife, Maggie, who came over. Alice gave them the news in the living room that holds so many rich family memories.

After raising her five children here, and following Tom's death, Alice allowed part of the house to be used as a temporary shelter for the homeless. The Horton house was redone with wheelchair ramps (installed by Roman with the help of several others) and a separate entrance.

Wendy lived here shortly after Benjamin was born. Kristen worked as a social worker here for a while when she first arrived in Salem. For most of 1996–97, Alice, Hope, and Shawn-Douglas lived in the main part of the house.

When Hope found a marijuana joint in Shawn-D's backpack, she embarked on a personal battle against drugs that almost brought her too close to Bo's under-cover operation. A few months later, Billie (who was involved with Bo's work) dropped some pills Max gave her. She picked them up but missed one, and when an investigator questioning Shawn-D's shooting thought it was the boy's, Billie spoke up and Hope thought Billie was back on drugs.

When J. L. King thought Bo had betrayed him, he and Max set a bomb at the Horton house while Alice, Hope, and Shawn-D were inside. With no time to spare, Bo managed to get free of J. L. and diffused it.

An emotional explosion took its toll when Bo was about to tell Hope that he slept with Billie, but before he could, Hope told him that Billie was pregnant. It was over between them.

Alice Horton

Born in Salem to a blue-collar family, Alice became not only Tom's high school sweetheart but his only true love. The couple had five children: Tommy, Addie, Bill, Mickey, and Marie. A loving woman, devoted to her husband and family, Alice was and remains the quintessential mother and homemaker. Her trademark is unconditional love and loyalty to her family. After her children and grandchildren left the house, Alice became the Director of Volunteers at University Hospital. When the Community Center burned down several years ago, she convinced Tom to open up their home as a community center. She was devastated by Tom's death in 1994 after more than fifty years of marriage, but her faith in God and personal courage have seen her through. Alice continues to lend a kind ear, loving heart, and sage advice to family and friends who surround her.

Alice Horton remains the matriarch of the Horton family and is a loving friend to many more in Salem.

Tom Horton (1910–1994)

Still remembered in Salem as a patriarch and well-loved citizen, family man, and friend, Tom Horton lived and died in Salem. In his youth, he dated Alice Grayson in high school and married her shortly after she graduated a year behind him. He played baseball with a local minor league team before completing his military duty and becoming a doctor like his dad had been. His grandson, Dr. Mike Horton, continues his professional and community commitment as Chief of Staff at the Salem University Medical Center, as was Tom. Alice is joined by loving family members every Christmas as they hang the traditional Horton ornaments, each with an individual's name on it. Alive or departed, in Salem or on the other side of the globe, all Hortons are celebrated on that special day each year, and none more than Tom, whose love was limitless.

Mickey Horton

For a long time the bachelor of the family, this lawyer fell for his brother Bill's fiancée, Dr. Laura Spencer, and won her love when she thought Bill had given up on her. They married, and for years Mickey thought he was father to their child, Mike. However, he was really the boy's uncle and Bill was the dad. A heart attack and ensuing stroke left Mickey with amnesia and he lived another life, and found another wife, Maggie Simmons. When he did learn Mike was not his son, Mickey had an emotional collapse, shot and wounded Bill, and was committed for psychiatric help for several months.

With Maggie, he was foster parent to Melissa Anderson and adopted Sarah Horton, Maggie's child by insemination. Both grown children now live in Nashville. Like several others in Salem, Mickey was once held captive by Stefano DiMera. During that time, he was presumed dead. When he returned, he and Maggie divorced, then remarried (for the third time!). Mickey is currently his mom, Alice's, main emotional support and busy defense lawyer for many Salem residents.

Since Tom's death, Mickey and Maggie have spent much more time visiting the original Horton homestead rather than entertaining in their own house across town.

Maggie Horton

She was a disabled and orphaned farm girl when Mickey stumbled through his amnesiac haze to her doorstep. Once in her Prince Charming's arms, Maggie found the medical help she needed to walk again, but emotional pressures (moving to Salem, Mickey's true identity, issues around motherhood, and having a foster child taken away) led her through a tough bout with alcohol, which she eventually overcame.

During Mickey's abduction by Stefano, he was presumed dead. Maggie and Don Craig nearly married. She also had romantic attention from Dr. Neil Curtis, who turned out to be the sperm donor of her child, Sarah. Maggie is the head of the Salem Arts Council and also volunteers at the hospital. With Alice, Maggie has investment in Billie's cosmetic company, Countess Wilhelmina. On the home front, she and Mickey have settled into married midlife contentment.

Hope Williams Brady

Hope's mom, Addie Horton Williams, was killed by a speeding car as she pushed Hope's carriage out of its way. Hope was raised by her dad, Doug, a local cabaret owner and performer, and her half-sister, Julie, who became her stepmom when she married Doug. As a teenager, Hope attended boarding school. When she came back to Salem, in 1984, she was a young adult with a stubborn streak surpassed only by her need for adventure. She met her match in Bo Brady. The two fell in love, but it has always been a bumpy road. On her eighteenth birthday, when her dad found her about to make love to Bo, Doug had a heart attack. Later that year, to protect Bo from harm, she was forced to marry corrupt D.A. Larry Welch. While caught up in the crime adventure surrounding the powerful prisms, Bo and Hope made love for the first time in the Oak Alley plantation house.

The following year, the duo joined ISA cohorts to chase down the Dragon. As a reward for their good work, Bo and Hope were given a grand wedding fit for a king and queen. Even their friends and family were flown to England. In 1987, after many crime-fighting adventures and the birth of their son, Shawn-Douglas, Bo and Hope decided to go on a private adventure. They bought a boat and the threesome sailed away. When they eventually returned to Salem, it was a short stay. After a dangerous adventure during the Cruise of Deception, Hope was presumed dead in a fiery explosion in 1991. However, after many twists and turns through forgotten years with Stefano DiMera, Hope returned to Salem in 1994. Her presence and returned memory eventually brought an end to Bo's marriage to

Billie. Then after Franco worked his manipulation and drug lord J. L. King forced a marriage between Bo and Billie, Hope was again on her own. Still feisty after all these years, Hope had adventures in the jungle with John and in the Southern bayou before more of her missing years' memories were recaptured.

Hope Brady lived with her great-grandmother while Bo was torn between his love for Hope and responsibility to Billie.

DID YOU KNOW:

She was named Hope, as in "new hope," because her mother, Addie, had cancer while pregnant.

❧

Hope went to Lincoln High School.

❧

Bo called her Fancy Face because of the makeup she wore to impress him.

❧

Before becoming a model she was a police officer and private investigator.

❧

Bo's words at Hope's memorial service after she was lost in an avalanche and thought dead:

I finally agreed to a memorial service for Hope. I still can't believe that she's gone. To be so close to having her back and then to have her taken away . . . the pain is almost unbearable. The first time I lost her was hard enough, but this time, this time is much worse. I should have been there for her. If I'd just told her that I loved her, she might not have gone up on that mountain to ski, or at least we would have been there together and I could have been there with her. Now I've lost her and I'll never be able to forgive myself.

❧

Shawn-Douglas Brady

Bo and Hope's son was born in 1987. Soon after his arrival, his parents bought a boat and the threesome took off for a three-year world cruise. He's been through some rough times coping with Bo and Hope's estrangements and reconciliations, but he's a resilient youngster. He was also a very lucky one when he survived a gunshot wound by a teenage drug-runner working for J. L. King in 1997.

Shawn-Douglas, like mom Hope, enjoyed Alice's companionship and warm home, but wanted a stable home with loving parents sharing a family life.

Horton Cabin on Smith Island

At one time, Smith Island was actually a peninsula with a narrow strip of land keeping it attached to the mainland; Bo was still able to ride his motorcycle across it. Over time, the peninsula eroded and created a true island. A ferry and private boats connect mainland people to it now. There are only a handful of cabins there, but none have phone service.

There are small groups of cabins dispersed over the island. It's very desolate without electricity, and showers are outside so it feels primitive, like a summer camp. It was the family vacation cabin for longer than Alice and Tom were married. It's filled with family photos.

At the start of their relationship many years back, Bo and Hope carved their initials in a heart on a tree near the dock on the island. They used to picnic there frequently in the early eighties.

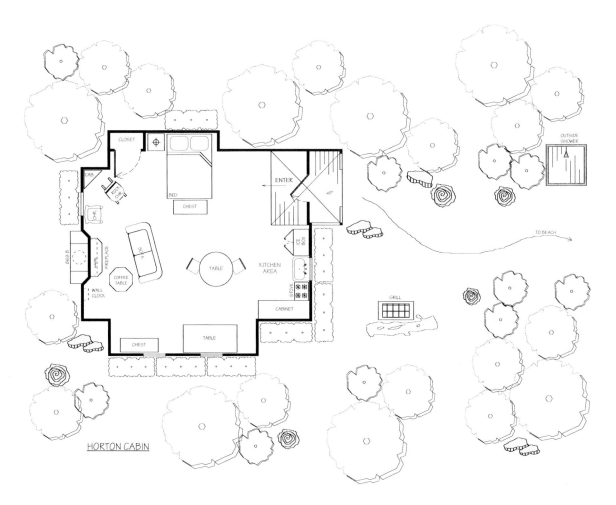

HORTON CABIN

In fall 1993, Marlena gave birth to Isabella (Belle) Brady with John and Kristen assisting her.

Bo and Hope with Billie and Franco once enjoyed a double date on the island until Andre secretly showed up and confronted Franco about what he was up to in Salem. Before the end of the day, Andre was found dead by Billie.

In the spring of 1996, Bo and Hope made love at the Horton cabin for the first time since Hope returned to Salem after she was thought dead in 1990. Bo also proposed marriage.

In November, the night before Bo and Hope's second wedding, Billie went to the cabin rather than torture herself at the ceremony and reception. When Bo found out she was headed off alone, he went to the island to check on her. Franco secretly managed to get Bo stranded there. When his attempt to swim ashore failed, Billie rescued him from the frigid water. Back at the cabin, he fell asleep in front of the fireplace with Billie snuggling to keep him warm. That's where Hope found them when she left the church to look for her groom.

In the fall of 1997, Roman brought Marlena here for a special lunch. A bit too anxious to be up and around after his illness, Roman suffered convulsions, but Marlena saved him and got him back to the mainland and the hospital.

The Homes of Salem   19

*On Horton Island the lagoon
always offered Bo and Hope a
private retreat for special romantic
moments.*

*Every Christmas family members hang ornaments
with names for each member of the Horton family.
Mike remembers his son, Jeremy, who lives with his
mom, Robin, in Israel, and Maggie always hangs
ornaments with Sarah's and Melissa's names on them.*

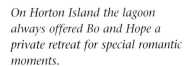

*Lucas was born out of an affair between Mike Horton's
dad and Kate Roberts. The news was a shock to
everyone in Salem and took some getting used to
between the half-brothers.*

Fancy Face, Bo Brady's Boat

PIER 58

This Cal25 with customized interior was destroyed by fire in 1997. Bo had almost a lifetime of memories on the boat, *Fancy Face,* which he had given the nickname he'd called Hope, his true love. Bo, Hope, and their son, Shawn-Douglas, cruised around the world on this seaworthy vessel.

After it seemed Hope had been killed in 1990, Bo lived on the boat. Much later, he spent a lot of romantic time with Dr. Carly Manning on the boat too. The *Fancy Face* was his home while he was also involved with Billie, but when Hope "returned from the dead," it was again their special place—but perhaps, never really the same.

In early 1996, Bo was depressed over losing Hope yet again in an avalanche and took dangerous police chases to distract himself. He also spent quiet time on the boat. When the bell seemed to ring mysteriously, Bo was convinced Hope was still alive and renewed his search.

Reunited, Bo proposed to Hope for the second time in their lives. As they planned their wedding, Bo promised to buy her the house she had always wanted.

After the wedding day proved disastrous, and Hope was off to Santa Rosa on a photo shoot with Franco, Bo lost the *Fancy Face* in a gambling bet.

When it seemed Bo could get the boat back, the *Fancy Face* was mysteriously burned, completely destroyed. An important chapter in Bo and Hope's lives was closed.

Bo Brady

This Brady is actually the biological son of Victor Kiriakis, who had a brief affair with Bo's mom, Caroline. Over the years, especially through Bo's adolescence and early adulthood, Bo and dad Shawn often felt an instinctual tension in their relationship. After the long-ago affair and paternity were acknowledged, the two realized they had more in common than not and quietly reconciled their differences.

Attractive to many ladies in Salem, this motorcycle-riding, ex–Merchant Marine had one great love, Hope Williams, whom he fell for when she was just seventeen. After they shared many crime-fighting adventures, and together had a son, Shawn-Douglas, Hope was presumed killed in 1987.

No matter who else shared moments on the Fancy Face, *it remained always and forever haunted by the Fancy Face it was named for—Hope.*

After reconciling with that loss, Bo nearly married Dr. Carly Manning, then became involved with former prostitute and drug addict Billie Reed. It was only after they wed that Hope-look-alike Gina was determined to really be Hope. Billie left town and Bo and Hope spent about a year reestablishing their love. Just before their rewedding, Billie came back to Salem, and because of some secret manipulations by Franco, Bo and Hope never made it to the altar. Then, during an undercover drug operation, Bo was forced to marry Billie. The marriage would have been annulled had it not been, first, for Billie's bout with drugs and, second, her pregnancy, which ended in a miscarriage. Bo stayed with Billie because of his sense of responsibility and guilt. However, Bo and Hope are lovers who can never stay apart for very long.

Bo's poem to Hope 1/15/96:

She looks at the world
through eyes of kindness,
her hair glistens with the brilliant
glow of stars,
her face reflecting certainty and
expectation.
Faith and hope turn always to the
light.
And her lips touch our souls with
kisses
too sweet to remember without tears
of joy.
She stands cloaked in warmth and
tenderness and mystery.
She is love, precious love,
to the fortunate she comes once,
but never again,
so guard her with every strength in
you
never let her go.

DID YOU KNOW:

The motto for Brady and Brady, Bo and Hope's private investigation company, was "If no one can, we can."

Bo has a dagger tattoo on his shoulder. During his Merchant Marine days he, Steve, and Britta had them done as part of a friendship-forever gesture.

He graduated from Salem High School and his favorite color is blue.

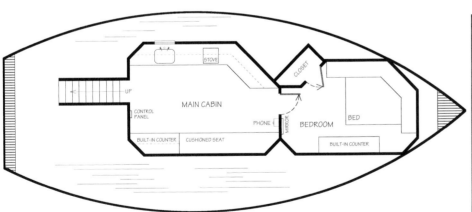

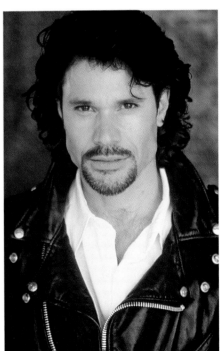

An unconventional fellow, Bo was always more comfortable on the back of his motorcycle or on his boat than in a house with a garden and picket fence.

Brady Home

48 WATER STREET

Brady Pub

48 RIVER STREET

One of the more unique properties in Salem, the Brady Pub is on a street against a hillside; the Brady residence is above the pub with the home's entrance at hilltop level.

After commercial fisherman Shawn retired, he started a family-run business, a fish market. Almost a decade later in 1992 when robbers vandalized the fish market, Shawn was shot. That incident caused Bo to become a policeman.

John Black, who had become a member of the family when wrongly thought to be Roman for several years, financed the new venture, the Brady Pub, which immediately became a popular social haven. There are plenty of parties and impromptu song fests. The pub also has a kitchen off the bar. The Irish-pub-style eatery has an East Coast feel: not big, but very cozy and friendly.

Shawn and Caroline's home is above the pub. There is a staircase from the pub that goes directly upstairs to their kitchen and family room. Another entrance is found from the hilltop street that is behind and above the pub. The dwelling is built on a multilevel piece of property that allows separate access to the residence and also explains why there are two addresses.

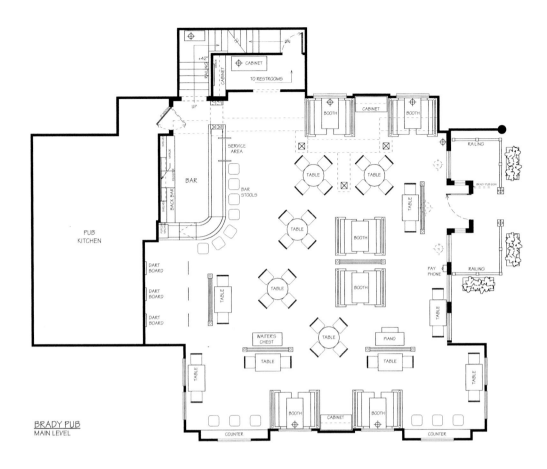

BRADY PUB
MAIN LEVEL

Labels within main level:
CABINET
TO RESTROOMS
+42"
RAILING
CABINET
UP
DN
BOOTH
CABINET
BOOTH
RAILING
BRADY PUB SIGN
SERVICE AREA
BAR
BAR STOOLS
TABLE
TABLE
BACK BAR
TABLE
PUB KITCHEN
TABLE
TABLE
BOOTH
PAY PHONE
RAILING
DART BOARD
DART BOARD
DART BOARD
TABLE
TABLE
BOOTH
TABLE
WAITER'S CHEST
TABLE
PIANO
TABLE
TABLE
TABLE
BOOTH
CABINET
BOOTH
TABLE
COUNTER
COUNTER

BRADY PUB
SECOND LEVEL

Labels within second level:
DN
+42"
RAILING
CABINET
UP
BATHROOM
CORRIDOR
TABLE
SECOND LEVEL PATIO
CLOSET
BED
BEDROOM
CHEST
CLOCK
FIREPLACE
MANTEL
CABINET
CHEST
WASHER
DRYER
LAUNDRY
RUG
RUG
TV
CHAIR
+6"
BOOKCASES
BEDROOM
CHEST
CHEST
BED
BED
BENCH
BAKER'S RACK
LIVING ROOM
TABLE
TABLE
MASTER BEDROOM
CLOSET
BOOKCASE
TABLE
BATHROOM
KITCHEN
WORK TABLE
PANTRY
REF.

The kitchen-family room of the house is the main gathering space. The residence is actually bigger in area than the pub beneath it because of the odd dimensions of the lots. When one enters the Brady home from the residence level, it's larger, spreading out atop the hillside. The house has three bedrooms and several baths.

In early 1998, Jennifer's post-funeral reception turned into a celebration as she turned out to be very much alive and well. Meanwhile, Bo and Hope made their way upstairs to the Brady family room to have a private talk. Billie came up too, just in time to hear Bo say he wished Billie were not pregnant. Billie was shocked to tears and went home.

Once upstairs at the Brady house, the cozy living room and adjacent kitchen open up to a surprising floor plan of several bedrooms for family and guests.

The pub downstairs becomes an enormous "family room" where Salem residents gather in times of joy and sorrow, and everyday cordiality.

Caroline Brady

She's the matriarch of the Brady clan, a family of blue-collar, hardworking people with no airs about them. They're generally more outspoken and emotionally expressive than the comparatively conservative Horton family. Yet they share solid family values and outlook. Caroline is a feisty woman who will stand up to anyone for the good of her family.

She's very human, not without her shortcomings. In the early days of her marriage, Caroline had an affair with Victor Kiriakis and gave birth to Bo, her second son. She kept that secret for many years, until Victor returned to Salem in 1985. He wanted to renew their relationship, but she refused. He pressured her, but she stood up to him, even threatening him with a gun if he tried to interfere with her family. Of course, it was at that moment that Bo entered the hotel room with his gun drawn. When Caroline shouted at him not to shoot, not to hurt his father, Bo learned the family secret.

Somehow, through prayer and love, Caroline and Shawn stayed married. Things healed between Shawn and Bo; their relationship had been pretty brittle, but neither knew why before the revelation. It was something they sensed. Their relationship has grown even more solid since.

Caroline spends her time sharing duties at the Brady Pub and baby-sitting her grandchildren. She's always a willing ear and offers a consoling shoulder to lean on for friends and family. She

---

DID YOU KNOW:

Her favorite novel
is *Pride and Prejudice*.

⌒〰〰〰〜

When she's nervous or upset,
she polishes the silverware.

⌒〰〰〰〜

She celebrates the anniversary
of Shawn's marriage proposal
every year.

---

nearly found herself victim of Vivian Alamain's mad revenge against Dr. Carly Manning when she was admitted to the hospital with a heart problem. Vivian had been killing Manning's patients.

Her religious faith helped to keep her safe in mind, spirit, and body when she assisted John during Marlena's exorcism.

Shawn Brady

The kindhearted, blustery Irish fisherman who married Caroline opened and ran a fish market so he could spend more time with his wife and family. After a robbery at the market, John helped the Bradys turn the store into the Brady Pub, where he's well-known for his homemade clam chowder.

Although Bo was the biological son of Victor Kiriakis, Shawn raised Bo, and the two are truly father and son in every other way. Shawn is biological father to other children with Caroline: Roman, Kimberly, and Kayla. The couple took in foster children Frankie and Max in the mid-eighties. They have grandchildren: Andrew and Jeannie Donovan; Stephanie Johnson; Carrie, Sami, Eric, and Shawn-Douglas Brady. They're honorary grandparents of Brady Black and Belle, both fathered by John Black, who was mistakenly thought to be Roman during the time Stefano held the real Roman captive.

Shawn is a devoted family man and loves the pub, where he parties with the best of his patrons and sings up a storm whenever he can.

> **DID YOU KNOW:**
>
> Shawn drives an older white Ford Explorer with the Brady Pub logo on the doors.
>
> ⌘
>
> He considers nightcrawlers the best bait to use when fishing off the pier.
>
> ⌘
>
> He married Caroline in 1948.

John Black's Loft

25 RIVER STREET

This residence is located in a renovated warehouse building with an outside elevator. It's in a nontraditional neighborhood popular with artists, writers, and actors. It has been a home to many over the years, including Kayla, Jennifer, Isabella, Bo, Hope, and Diana. John sold it in late 1997.

When John and Isabella lived there, Isabella brought a number of feminine touches with her. She liked wicker overstuffed chairs and a few blankets thrown over the furniture.

The last time Isabella, suffering from pancreatic cancer, left the loft, she and John were on their way to Italy. As the couple left their home, Isabella turned around at the staircase and said, "What a lovely room." The intonation, the quality of her words conveyed what everyone knew. She would not be back to a place that had brought her heart such great warmth and happiness. Isabella died in her homeland, Italy, in John's loving arms.

After her death, some of the paintings and graphics on the wall changed. Although John always treasured Isabella's memory, he brought back some of the masculine feel to the decor, replacing the floral still-life paintings with outdoor scenery of mountains and streams.

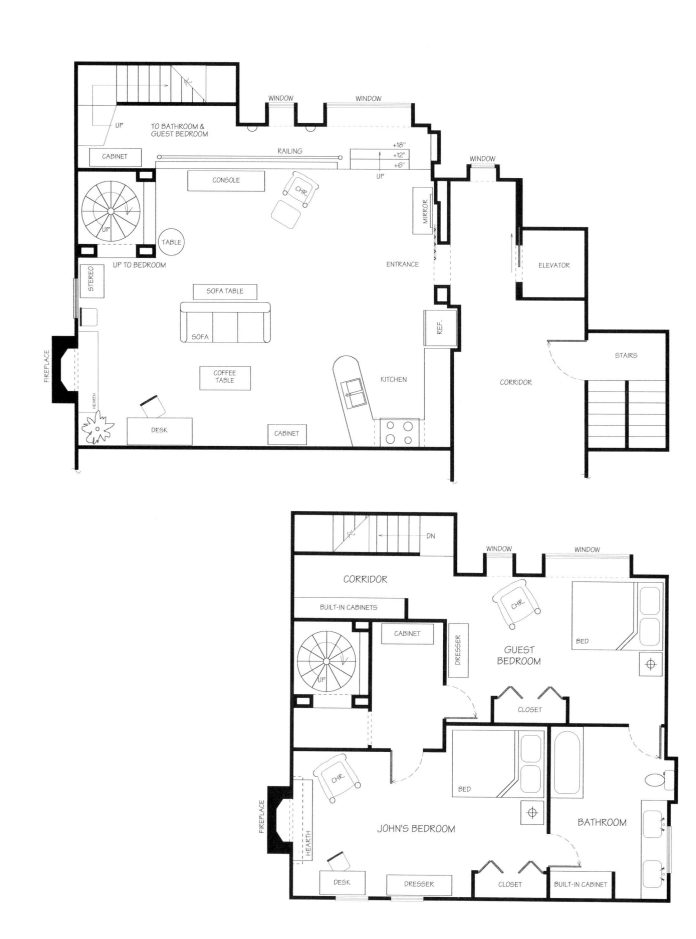

John Black

Roman Brady was thought to have been killed by Stefano, so when a mysterious man first arrived in Salem in 1986, no one imagined there could be a connection. However, as Dr. Marlena Evans started to work with this man who suffered amnesia and had recently undergone extensive cosmetic surgery, bits and pieces of information formed some disturbing patterns. At one point she thought he could be the evil Phoenix because of a tattoo on his shoulder. Then, after a visit to a surgeon who had photos of Roman in his files, Marlena was convinced that the man was none other than her husband. He moved into her house, her bed, and her heart. He picked up parenting duties for Roman's daughter Carrie and the twins, Sami and Eric.

After this man lived in Salem as Roman for about five years, the real Roman escaped from captivity and returned home. The man without a past assumed the name John Black. John later learned more of his own history in 1992 when Lawrence Alamain's aunt Vivian came to Salem. It turned out that John Black was really Forrest, Lawrence's presumed-dead brother. Once his inheritance was properly reimbursed from Vivian, who had claimed Forrest's inheritance, John had an independent income for life.

He got involved with Isabella Toscano, who became pregnant with his child about the time Danielle Stevens came to Salem claiming to be John's wife and a private investigator on the trail of jewel thief Romulus. She led him off to Europe and would have seduced him, but Isabella discovered Danielle was Romulus. John allowed Danielle to escape, then returned to Salem and wed Isabella. Their son, Brady Black, however, was born in a church anteroom before the couple exchanged wedding vows. Tragically, a few months later, Isabella died of pancreatic cancer in John's arms.

John never stopped loving Marlena, the woman who dominated his short remembered history. Even though they acknowledged their love for each other after Roman's return, Marlena was faithful to her husband and dedicated to her family. However, when John announced that he was leaving Salem for good, Marlena succumbed to a moment of passion aboard his private jet. That changed everything. John decided to stay in Salem and Marlena found out she had conceived, but was not certain if the father was Roman or John.

While Marlena was pregnant, John began a love affair with Kristen Blake, who turned out to be already betrothed to Tony DiMera. While John and Kristen embarked on their bumpy romance, Marlena delivered a baby girl, Belle. After the true paternity of the child came to light, Kristen felt betrayed and married Tony as planned. Then Stefano captured John and tortured him in a dungeon at Maison Blanche. Marlena tried to seduce DiMera to help John escape. Roman got them both out, then decided to divorce Marlena, and left town with a broken heart.

By then, John was committed to Kristen even though she was married to Tony. They could not continue their affair, however, because John discovered another piece of his past: He was a priest. That served Marlena well. When it became apparent that she was possessed by the devil, she needed to be exorcised and John did the job. John freed her of Satan and then freed himself of his priestly vows.

He and Kristen planned to find a way to be together, but before Kristen could obtain an annulment, fatally ill Tony committed suicide and, in a complex plot, framed John for murder. John was convicted and sentenced to death. He actually inhaled some fumes in the gas chamber before his innocence, revealed through Tony's diary, ironically saved him.

Marlena and John almost reunited, but Kristen became pregnant and John proposed marriage. Marlena refused to come between the couple for fear Kristen would miscarry. Kristen lost the baby anyway, but with the help of Stefano, a look-alike delivered a child Kristen passed off as her and John's infant.

Eventually, that ploy became unraveled, as did Kristen's fragile emotional instability. Once Kristen's lies and manipulations came to light, John and Marlena were free to marry and almost did until Roman, who was again thought dead in the course of an ISA mission, was returned to Salem by Kristen on what would have been John and Marlena's wedding day.

A hero under any circumstances, John trekked through the jungle to retrieve a cure for Roman's otherwise fatal illness. It looked as if Marlena and Roman would reunite, but the truth finally won out, Roman stepped aside, and Marlena and John became engaged.

Roman's letters to Marlena and John as he prepares to die:

Dear Doc,

If you're reading this, then I'm dead. I'm sorry for the pain you're feeling right now. I know despite the way things ended up between us, that you did love me, and I always loved you, Doc. I'm asking you for the sake of the love we shared to listen to my last request for you. I only pray that you will find the courage to grant me that request.

Doc, I know you did the best you could with a tough situation. After a lot of sleepless nights and days filled with thinking of you, I finally realized that you and John couldn't help the feelings you had for each other. In some ways I guess they were born out of your love for me.

After all, you thought John was me when you fell in love with him. It was a cruel trick of Stefano's. We were all his victims, Doc. So I just wanted you to know that I don't hold you or John responsible for your affair. Both of you are quality people, people whom I value and love. John is a decent man. When I came back, he stepped aside and let us be together. That took a lot of strength. I don't know if I would have able to walk away from you in the same circumstances. But I understand that you both must have been drawn back to each other. I have a feeling that you are still drawn to him. If you are, you should be with him. That is my last request to you, Doc, be with John and live out your love for him.

I give you and John my blessing, and I hope with all my heart that you two will find happiness in the love that I know you share for each other. You deserve it, Doc.

Doc, I can't imagine going on without you and I'm glad I don't have to anymore. It's better this way and I will truly be able to rest in peace if you take my words to heart.

I've gained a lot of wisdom these past few years. The one thing that was the hardest for me to see, to admit, was that you and John belong together. Maybe you always did. And if you can't be with me, I want you to be with him. I love you and want you to be happy. Please go to John and tell him you love him. I know he feels the same way about you. Do this for me, for the memory of the happiness we once shared. My love for you will live on past my death.

Remember me fondly,

Love, Roman

Dear John:

If you're reading this letter, it means I'm dead. I want to make sure there are no bad feelings left between us. I understand why things happened the way they did between you and Doc. I don't blame either of you. It took me a while to let go of my anger, but I know your affair was the result of a deep love you felt for each other when you both thought you were me. Stefano played with all our lives, all our emotions, but the bottom line is, I know how much you and Doc still love each other. I just pray that you won't let circumstances keep you from being together. She needs you, John, not only to console and comfort her, but to love her. I plead with you, do the right thing and, once again, make Doc your wife. Nothing would make me happier.

Roman

Marlena's Penthouse

24 RIVERVIEW DRIVE

This is the fourteenth-floor penthouse that John bought for Marlena and Belle after she and Roman separated in early 1994. Although it has been extensively remodeled, it is the same penthouse that once belonged to Julie Williams before she went to Europe to join Doug.

One piece of remodeling that Marlena did not know about was the secret door that Stefano had installed from the adjacent penthouse he acquired after Marlena moved into her unit. He managed somehow to create a passage through her standing closet into her bedroom. It was through this secret entrance that he visited Marlena in phantom-of-the-armoire fashion, taking her on nightly jaunts to faraway places. Whatever method Stefano used on Marlena, hypnosis or drugs, opened some other door—one to Marlena's spirit. Soon after, she became possessed by the devil.

After causing destruction and mayhem throughout Salem, the possessed Marlena was finally subdued and an exorcism was performed by John with the help of Caroline Brady and others in her own bedroom. Stefano even tried to face the demon himself, but was hurled from the bedroom window.

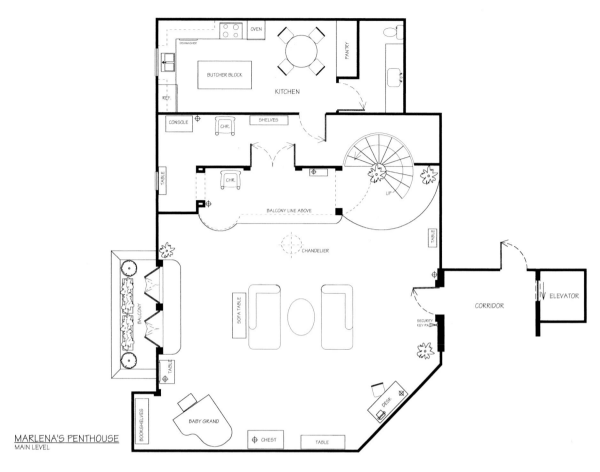

MARLENA'S PENTHOUSE
MAIN LEVEL

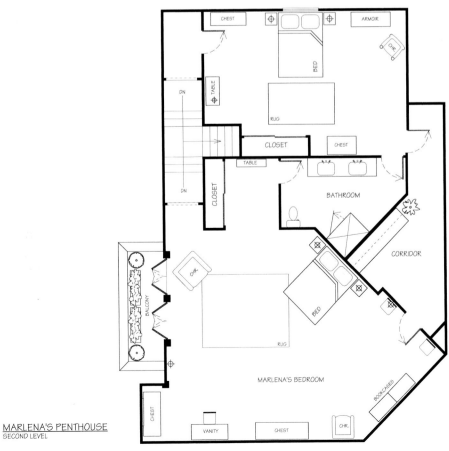

MARLENA'S PENTHOUSE
SECOND LEVEL

It might seem surprising that Marlena would still choose to live in this place of torment. However, after the exorcism, Marlena remembered nothing of the ordeal. Thankfully, sleeping in the same bedroom, she manages to have sweet dreams and peaceful sleep.

Marlena has replaced any memories of that time with others. Eric has returned to Salem and often visits his mother at the penthouse. John is back in her life and the two spend many romantic times together here.

When Susan Banks needed refuge, she and her baby, Elvis, stayed in the penthouse guest room. Later, Kristen, who sold Susan into white slavery and planned to steal baby Elvis, disguised herself as Susan and stayed at the penthouse too.

The Christmas of 1997 was a cheerful time. Eric and Sami created an old-fashioned Brady Christmas, hoping it would bring Marlena and Roman back together. When John mistakenly stopped by, Eric showed him the door.

Kristen's snooping through the penthouse gave her the information she needed to track down Susan. Excited to share a society-page item and photo, Susan had faxed a copy of the story to Marlena. When Kristen found it, she had all she needed to lead her to Susan.

Edmund surprised Susan by flying his mother Violet and baby Elvis to Salem. At the first opportunity, Kristen, in Susan disguise, drugged Violet and started to leave with Elvis. However, the baby developed an ear infection and could not fly.

Marlena Evans Brady

This well-respected psychiatrist is much loved by her many friends and family. She arrived in Salem to help treat Mickey Horton, who was institutionalized in 1976 after a mental-emotional collapse.

She found more danger and intrigue than she ever imagined in a comparatively small town at the time. Her jealous twin sister, Samantha, arrived from Denver, Colorado, shortly thereafter, then impersonated Marlena and had her institutionalized before her plot was uncovered. Marlena married lawyer Don Craig in 1980 but they lost their child to Sudden Infant Death Syndrome and they divorced shortly thereafter. While she was being stalked by the Salem Strangler, Detective

Marlena Evans has come a long way since arriving in Salem and first working at Bayview Sanitarium in 1976. Most people would not have survived the trials and traumas she's been through!

Today, Marlena lives in the style and sophistication appropriate to a woman of her professional stature. The penthouse, however, was a gift from John. Much of Marlena's life was disrupted by love-obsessed Stefano.

Roman Brady became her bodyguard and beau. They married, but shortly after she delivered their twins, Sami and Eric, Roman was shot and presumed killed by Stefano DiMera.

Marlena was kidnapped more than once by Stefano and other international criminals. She once thought she fatally shot Stefano, but he turned up alive again.

Marlena thought Roman was dead for several years before he seemed to return to Salem looking quite different and without a memory. She was delighted to have her husband home again and the two resumed married life. Later, it was a mixed blessing when

DID YOU KNOW:

Marlena loves to read Jane Austen classics and current mystery novels.

She used to drive a white Jeep Cherokee but now has a light-colored Mercedes-Benz sedan.

Her favorite sandwich is pastrami on rye.

the real Roman escaped his captivity and came back to Salem. They managed to pick up the pieces and the three—John, Roman, and Marlena—remained friends.

Aside from keeping her husbands straight, Marlena has had other challenges. In 1992 she was held captive in a boiler pit of an abandoned warehouse by a jealous, crazed Stella Lombard, who was convinced Marlena wanted her husband, Roger. John saved Marlena's life after the warehouse was demolished.

Marlena and John never stopped loving each other, but she chose to stay with her husband, Roman, and family. However, when John almost left Salem, they had a one-night tryst that produced baby Belle. When Belle's paternity became known, Roman divorced Marlena and left town. By then, John was committed to Kristen Blake.

Marlena next experienced greater jeopardy from Stefano, who took her for nightly excursions into his fantastic world of romantic delights. Unfortunately, the mental, emotional, and spiritual disruption left her open to demonic possession. She caused havoc for many friends and family in Salem before John, who turned out also to be a priest, performed an exorcism and saved her.

Before Marlena and Roman split, John started a love affair with Stefano DiMera's adopted daughter, Kristen. However, Kristen kept her promise and married Tony DiMera. Within a short time, Tony found out about her true feelings and had John framed for his suicide, which Tony orchestrated to look like murder. John never stopped loving Marlena. While he was on death row awaiting sentence, John wrote Marlena a love letter spilling all his long-pent-up emotions about her. Before she read it, Stefano managed to kidnap her yet again, and kept her in a gilded cage in a strange minikingdom below the streets of Paris. John rescued her again, but both believed the other could not return the feeling. And John was emotionally entangled with, and engaged to a pregnant Kristen.

Marlena kept secret her knowledge of Kristen's involvement in helping Stefano abduct her, for fear Kristen would miscarry John's baby. Marlena and John were unaware that Kristen had already miscarried and that Stefano hired a lookalike to deliver a child for her.

Once Kristen's lies and deceptions finally came to light, Marlena and John were free to wed. Just before they walked down the aisle, however, Kristen brought wheelchair-bound and previously presumed-dead Roman back to Salem. For months, Marlena, John, and Kristen played out their bogus roles as Roman regained his strength. Eventually, Roman learned the truth of John's relationship to Marlena. For a short time Roman tried to win Marlena back but gallantly bowed out of the triangle when he recognized John and Marlena's soul-mate bond.

The Blake House

PINE MOUNTAIN ROAD

Peter had this house built in Salem for himself and Jennifer. It is a replica of the Blake house in which he grew up in Aremid. That original Aremid home burned down in 1996. This current house is a new one built to look old, so the colors are a little fresher, but the decorating style is still very traditional, although a bit more high-end in price. There are primitive eighteenth-century American paintings, mostly of children, and heirloom American folk art highlights many rooms. There's a Pennsylvania Dutch grandfather clock in the foyer and a great number of Chippendale antiques throughout the mansion.

This residence is located on a hill of about an acre and is partially surrounded by woods. It is huge, with six bedrooms and even more baths. It has nautical elements in places, including a widow's walk. Otherwise, it's somewhat Victorian with a clapboard front. Although it has no tennis court, it most certainly has a pool, and a four-car garage separate from the house. There are separate unused servants' quarters.

There are a number of secret rooms. One opens from under the foyer staircase; another from behind a painting in the living room; and one more is off of one of the bedrooms. All are beautifully and very carefully concealed architecturally.

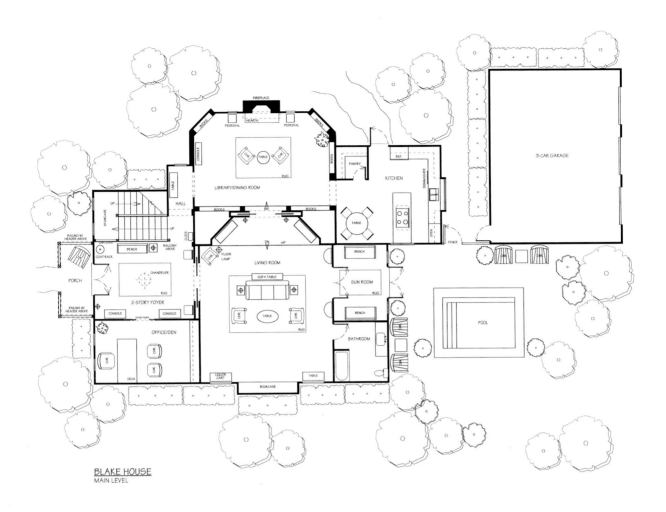

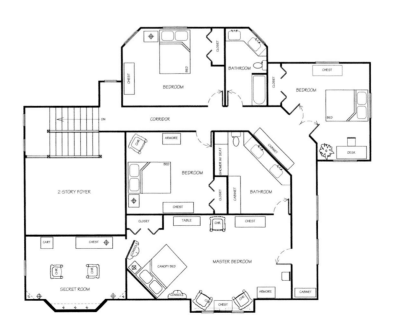

Peter hoped that he and Jennifer would be happy here. Unfortunately, Jennifer learned of his underhanded alter-ego and Peter was "killed" by Jack before the couple took up residence.

This is the house where Stefano and Peter, hiding out after Peter's supposed death, were confronted by Daniel Scott. Scott ended up falling from the second-floor window. He became the body that passed for Peter's at the funeral and burial.

After Laura stumbled upon the truth—that Peter was alive—she was held in a secret room here and given a laser treatment that erased her short-term memory. The secret room is accessible through the master bedroom behind a dresser. The room itself is an impressive work with acoustic panels making it soundproof, but it has a speaker system so that anything going on throughout the house can be monitored.

The Blake house became Kristen's haven and the site of another grandiose scheme. In order to kidnap baby Elvis, Kristen planned to sell Susan into slavery. Through an odd mix of events, all Salem believed Kristen was found dead in the Blake house pool. In fact, it was another Banks sibling, Penelope, killed somewhat accidentally and mistakenly by Edmund Crumb, Susan's fiancé. The Blake house "killing pool" mystery affected a number of lives in Salem when Dr. Laura became the prime suspect.

Kristen Blake DiMera

When she first came to Salem, Kristen was a social worker at the Horton Center and soon caught John's eye. While cleaning graffiti off walls and organizing youth baseball games, Kristen was the picture of wholesome selflessness. However, it eventually became known that Kristen was raised, with her brother Peter, by Stefano DiMera and was engaged to his son, Tony. Her presumed-dead mother turned up alive, but physically and emotionally scarred by DiMera machinations.

Kristen was tainted by her DiMera association too. She married Tony in 1994 but remained in love with John. After Tony's death, Kristen became pregnant by John but lost the baby. She continued the charade of pregnancy to keep him. A pregnant look-alike named Susan was hired to carry and deliver a child (later learned to have been fathered by Stefano) that would be passed off as Kristen's child. Susan proved to be a far more adept adversary than either Kristen or Stefano could ever have imagined. After Marlena uncovered all of Kristen's secrets and lies, and helped Susan get away from Salem, Kristen was all but ruined. Her chances with John certainly were. Later, she was presumed dead in the swimming pool of her home, sent Susan off in exile, and took on Susan's persona in hopes of getting away with baby Elvis. Tables were turned, however, when Susan escaped captivity, captured Kristen with the help of her fiancé, Edmund, and sent Kristen into secret exile, where she remains today.

The beautiful Kristen Blake arrived in Salem as a social worker with wealthy connections. As the adopted daughter of Stefano DiMera, her fate took her through an unhappy marriage to Tony DiMera and a badly twisted affair with John Black. Now she's believed dead by most in Salem. Stefano thinks she's happily traveling, but in fact, she's being held hostage by a perverse slave master. Some would say she's definitely gotten her just desserts.

DID YOU KNOW:

Her blood type is O.

❧

She likes to read historical Russian novels in Russian.

❧

She has a B.A. from Harvard and M.B.A. from Princeton.

❧

Her favorite childhood pet was a pony named Fudge.

The Apartment House

110 GUILFORD STREET

In a renovated building in a transitional part of town, the young adults of Salem have enjoyed sharing a sometimes awkward camaraderie. In a variety of situations, at one time or another, Austin, Carrie, Sami, Jonah, Wendy, and Eric have rented here.

The layouts of the studio, one-, and two-bedroom apartments are similar. For the most part, only color sets them apart. Originally, Carrie's was robin's-egg blue; Austin favored a masculine khaki shade; and Wendy liked pink.

CARRIE'S APARTMENT

When Carrie first moved into the building in 1992 it was more funky than trendy; she couldn't afford comfortable furniture and made do with lawn chairs. This was around the time she was infatuated with Jesse Lombard. As time went by, Carrie acquired more furniture and updated her place. Likewise, the neigh-

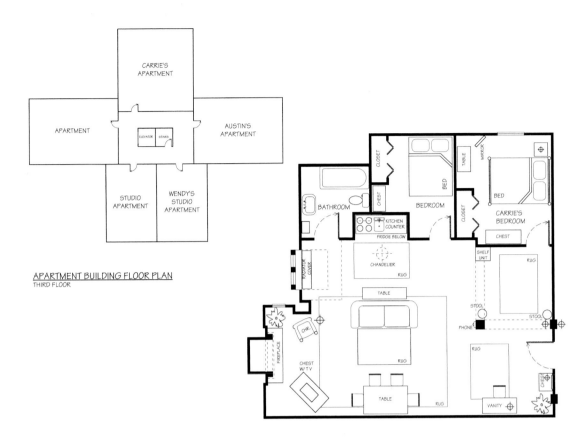

APARTMENT BUILDING FLOOR PLAN
THIRD FLOOR

CARRIE'S APARTMENT

WENDY'S STUDIO APARTMENT

AUSTIN'S APARTMENT

Carrie turned to Lucas as a friend and confidante when Sami had her hold on Austin. Lucas, however, played his part in many of Sami's plots hoping Carrie would eventually fall for him and forget Austin.

borhood became more polished, and trendy coffee shops, florists, and bookstores began to pop up.

In Carrie's bedroom, she and Lucas woke up together unaware of the night before. Sami drugged Carrie and dumped drunken Lucas beside her. Then Sami waited for Austin to discover them.

At the end of 1996, Billie was Carrie's roommate. When Billie watched videotapes of her and Bo during their happy time together, she broke down and cried. Bo happened by and comforted her, and watched the video too. It was a setup by Franco, who made sure Hope saw the couple "enjoying" their past times. Hope nearly canceled their wedding.

In the living room, Sami confronted Carrie over keeping Austin away from his son, Will, during the holiday season.

After Carrie married Austin and moved into his apartment, Eric took over Carrie's lease.

SAMI'S APARTMENT

Although in the same building as Carrie's, Sami's apartment was less desirable. She used the run-down condition of the flat to call Austin to repair leaking faucets, the failing air conditioner, and anything else she could conjure. Her ploys worked for a while but Austin caught on to her.

A seemingly maternal woman named Mary was Sami's neighbor and offered to baby-sit for Will. Sami never realized until too late that the woman had quite another plan in mind. After slipping Sami knockout drops in a drink, Mary kidnapped Will and took him to Europe, where she sold him on the black market. Luckily, the child was retrieved.

While Sami was hospitalized after Austin slammed her with his out-of-control car, both Kate and Vivian searched Sami's flat for the blackmail material she had on Kate. It was actually hidden in a doll Carrie brought to the hospital to comfort Sami, who had amnesia at that point.

Scheming Sami felt she was making headway with Austin, especially after he gave her one of his mother, Kate's, bracelets to wear at Kate's memorial.

AUSTIN'S APARTMENT

Austin's apartment, similar to others in the building, remained architecturally the same although several interior changes were made during the periods when he shared the place with Jonah, then with Sami and Will, and finally with Carrie.

After slipping him a drug at a bar, Sami, wearing Carrie's perfume, duped Austin into making love to her. In his state, he thought he was with Carrie. Sami didn't mind. When she later discovered she was pregnant, she happily assumed it was his child.

It was in Austin's kitchen that Sami created one of her first impressive meals for Austin. She prepared beef Wellington with Jamie's help, and dinner guest Lucas helped them eat it. The crème brûlée for dessert was a big hit.

On a short outing from the hospital, Lucas brought Sami to the apartment, where she saw a negligee and lipstick, Midnight Rose, that were not hers. She later accused Carrie of trying to steal Austin.

As a young father, Austin took his responsibilities seriously. However, the proximity of Carrie's apartment often made matters difficult as the couple saw each other daily.

Kate, using the situation to snoop for the blackmail material Sami held over her, totally renovated the apartment, making it wheelchair accessible and decorating it in more refined taste.

When Sami was released from the hospital, and still unable to walk, she and Will moved into Austin's apartment. She had the bedroom; he slept on the couch. Even when she asked him to spend the night, he started there, moved to the couch, and returned to Sami's bed in the morning.

Sami was nearly electrocuted when she tried to fix a faulty iron. The hair-raising shock brought back her memory, but she kept that a secret to use to her advantage.

Sami bought a computer for Austin, hoping it would help him work at home. It didn't work.

Austin found Sami in the living room with the annulment papers in her hand and came clean about his feelings for Carrie and the real circumstances of their own marriage. Sami, still pretending she didn't have her memory back, begged him not to leave her, then moved into the Kiriakis mansion.

After Austin and Carrie wed, the apartment was given a slicker, high-design look, befitting the atmosphere of a successful couple working at Titan. There are masculine touches that reflect Austin's interest in sports and an old pinball machine–front on the wall as decoration.

There are plenty of Countess Wilhelmena products for him and her on the vanity. This couple likes to take the time and effort to look good. There's also a whimsical rubber duckie in the tub.

WENDY'S APARTMENT

Wendy lived here with her son, Benjamin. Later, after she dated Jonah for a while, he moved in with her at the time Sami moved in with Austin.

While baby-sitting Benjamin, Lexie was nearly abducted by Stefano. She resisted him and called Abe, and Stefano was later jailed.

ON THE ROOF . . .

Austin and Jennifer bonded on the roof, each talking about their loves and dreams. He was working at the station with Jennifer at the time. They became good friends.

At the strike of the new year, Austin and Carrie were to meet on the rooftop signaling their willingness to renew their relationship. Sami managed to change the clock so that Austin and Carrie arrived at different times, each believing the other was no longer interested.

When Austin and Carrie returned from Paris, a surprise party awaited them there. A large welcoming banner that read "Carrie and Austin—Together Forever!" tore at their hearts. Because of complications in getting French officials to release Will to return to the States, the child's birth parents—Sami and Austin—had to marry before leaving Paris.

Apartment rooftop celebration of Will's return

"I Love You Always Forever"

"I'll Make Love to You"

"Don't Let Go"
(Carrie and Austin dance; Bo remembers Billie)

Carrie Brady

The daughter of Roman Brady and his first wife, Anna, Carrie was raised by step-mom Marlena. Austin Reed and Carrie fell in love but met with obstacles to their relationship time and time again.

Roman came between them after Austin's street-kid past led to an acid burn on Carrie's face on the same night she became a finalist in the "Face of the Nineties" contest. Her physical and emotional scars were corrected, but it was almost a year

Carrie shared a hotel suite with Mike during a business trip, and he happened into her hotel bridal suite on the night she wed Austin. Carrie didn't realize her feelings for Mike until after her marriage started to feel neglected. Carrie was involved in her career and working closely with Mike, and Austin was caught up in Sami's and Will's troubles.

before the lovers reconciled. Then Carrie was nearly raped by an intruder, who then turned his attention on Sami. Alan seduced and date-raped Sami, who blamed Carrie for the rape and public humiliation when she pressed charges. Determined to get Austin, Sami drugged him and took him into her bed. Months later, that one-night stand destroyed Carrie's wedding when Sami used the occasion to announce she was pregnant by the groom.

Carrie and Austin since learned of Sami's manipulations; however, Austin's fatherly dedication to Will kept him all too often at Sami's side. Carrie's second wedding day with Austin was ruined by Sami, who became the bride herself! After an eventual annulment, Carrie and Austin were free to wed, but Austin felt obligated to Sami and Will. On their wedding day, Carrie found proof Will is not Austin's son, and Carrie and Austin were finally wed. They moved into Carrie's old apartment and started their married life together. Carrie landed a high-profile and demanding job at Titan in public relations. One of her assignments, Dr. Mike Horton, kept her busy and away from home as Austin renewed an interest in boxing. Carrie, meanwhile, found her interest in Mike was more than professional.

⁀౻

Roman's letter to Carrie as he lay dying:

Dear Carrie,

I didn't want anything to happen to me without telling you how much I love you and how proud I am that you are my firstborn child. You have such a kind heart, such intelligence and poise. Carrie, I know being the oldest child brings added responsibility—I know, I helped raise my younger brother and sisters—and that you are always there for Sami and Eric. You were the one constant in their lives when I was taken away from you and then Marlena. That's why I worry for them. They're not as independent as you are, Carrie. Or as strong. Especially Sami. I think she suffered the most when I came back. She felt so guilty about her feelings for John, and then Marlena's affair with John, and the divorce. It was too much for her. And it saddens me to think now that Sami finds it difficult to really trust anyone, except you. Sami's always looked up to you, Carrie, trusted you. And it gives me peace of mind to know that my daughters will always be close and that you'll always protect Sami. You're my legacy, Carrie. I know that you'll never betray your ideals and your essential goodness.

I love you, Pumpkin, forever and always,

Dad

⁀౻

Austin Reed

Although from a broken family with an abusive, drug-addicted father, Austin always had good values, a sense of loyalty, and soon won the respect of many people in Salem shortly after arriving in 1992. He also fell in love with Carrie Brady. The two faced many tests even from the start. Austin's presumed-dead father, Curtis, made a sudden reappearance and then was killed; Austin's sister, Billie, was put on trial for murder; Kate Roberts turned out to be his mother; his half-brother, Lucas, was resentful over no longer being the only son, and he had his own romantic interest in Carrie. Austin and Carrie made it to the altar, but before vows were exchanged, Sami announced Austin was the father of her unborn child. Through masterful scheming, Sami managed to keep Austin close, and eventually married him for a while. But now Austin and Carrie are married and trying to balance their lives, careers, and love.

DID YOU KNOW:

During his first boxing days he was called "Boston" Austin Reed.

ᏬᎿᏬ

He donated his bone marrow for Abby Deveraux in August 1993, and saved the little girl's life.

ᏬᎿᏬ

He met Carrie when she asked him to turn down the music playing in his apartment.

ᏬᎿᏬ

For Christmas 1992, Austin sold his record collection to buy back a diamond earring Carrie had pawned to pay her rent; she sold the matching diamond earring to buy Austin a record player for his jazz albums.

Austin was a boxer when he arrived in Salem but gave up the sport for Carrie. Now married to her, he's headed back to the ring.

Eric Brady

The other Brady twin decided to stay in Denver after graduating high school and went to college there while his sister Sami came back to Salem earlier. In 1997, Eric returned in time to find his father, Roman, whom he thought was dead, battling for his life, and his mother, Marlena, in a heated triangle between Roman and John. His sister Sami was up to her eyes in trouble too, but to this day he doesn't know the extent of her manipulations. However, Sami did land Eric a job as one of Titan's top fashion photographers and placed him in close contact with Nicole, the waitress-turned-model he first noticed at the Java Café. Eric didn't know that Nicole had a husband, or a good-looking sister too. This Brady boy has plenty of love trouble!

DID YOU KNOW:

Eric and his twin, Sami, went to grade school at Lakeside Elementary School.

◈

His middle name is Roman; his first name comes from his paternal grandfather's brother, Eric.

Eric is Sami's twin but even he was tricked by her devious ways. Soon after Eric arrived in town, he saw Sami scheme her way from the apartments to the Kiriakis mansion and an important position with Titan.

After returning to Salem, Eric became good pals with another bachelor, Mike Horton. After Austin and Carrie married and moved into Austin's apartment, Eric took Carrie's apartment.

The Carver House

Although not in the best part of town, it's not the worst area either. The immediate three-block area is very nice, but the neighborhood has changed enough to make Lexie think twice about raising a family here. Yet, it is the only house the Carvers have known for as long as Abe can remember. It's an old, large, two-story house that Abe either inherited or bought from his retired, still-living parents. The elder Carvers have a small apartment in Salem but enjoy traveling a great deal.

The house was originally a smaller Craftsman-style two-bedroom abode built around 1890. It grew with extensions and impressive renovations; even the garage went from one- to two-car size. Presently, there are three bedrooms and two baths.

Lexie has added chic and sophisticated touches while keeping Abe's taste and memories in mind. Lots of purple flowers, Lexie's favorite color, abound.

ABE & LEXIE CARVER'S HOUSE

Abe's favorite room is the bedroom, where he and Lexie really relax, spending quality time talking about important things and sometimes sipping champagne. Abe also likes his den, where he keeps many souvenirs, including the football used when his college, Salem University, won the championship. He also has medals for courage and commendations from the Salem police force. His bookshelves hold law enforcement books, popular best-sellers, nonfiction, history, and classics. There's a TV set in his den and another in the family room.

The kitchen is not the most important room in the house. The Carvers do a lot of take-out because both Lexie and Abe are busy career people with often conflicting schedules. Their favorite fare is Chinese food from Lu's restaurant.

Abe and Lexie share the household chores, without any set system or breakdown, rather than hire a housekeeper. They just take time on Saturday and do whatever needs to be done. This also includes garden tasks. Both love lots of well-kept seasonal flowers, and decorating for Christmas, their favorite holiday.

When Celeste came to Salem from Maison Blanche, she kept the secret of Lexie's parentage to herself. Lexie, however, started digging into her family past and discovered Aunt Frankie was actually her mother, Celeste.

These two crime fighters have joined forces in many adventures and share a deep and lasting friendship. When Marlena was last abducted by Stefano, Abe wasted no time joining John in coming up with a plan to rescue her.

Abe Carver

Abe was born and raised in Salem and always wanted to be a law-enforcement officer. That dedication was further bolstered after Theo died in his arms, shot by a corrupt Chief of Police. Abe vowed to fight corruption wherever he found it for the rest of his life.

Working in the Salem Police Department with Roman Brady, the two became the best of friends. Even when Roman returned and was so changed after being held captive by Stefano, their friendship was strong. Later, when the returned Roman turned out not to be Brady, but a brainwashed John Black, Abe found himself with two close buddies. The three remained as close as brothers and always had the common goal of bringing down Stefano and his evil influence in Salem and elsewhere.

Before Alexandra Brooks came into Abe's life, he thought of himself as a career bachelor with several women in his past. However, Lexie changed his point of view. There is no one else for Abe. The fact that Abe's wife and true love, Lexie, turned out to be the daughter of his worst enemy, Stefano, is ironic. Since that revelation, there have been many times when Abe has endured watching Lexie's emotions and loyalties pushed and pulled in several directions. He's often been saddened by the circumstance, and, on occasion, angered by his wife's choices. Still, their love and devotion is strong.

DID YOU KNOW:

Abe is the eldest of five siblings; he has two sisters who no longer live in Salem.

෨෴ල

Abe was once infatuated with Nikki Wade, a police secretary who was also interested in Abe's coworker, Danny Grant.

Abe and Lexie have a marriage built on lots of love and respect. Their two-career lifestyle keeps them community-focused, exciting individuals.

Lexie Carver

A former policewoman, Lexie lost her job after taking it upon herself to cover for her brother-in-law, Jonah Carver, who decided to become a part-time vigilante crime-fighter called the Pacifier. After being kicked out of the Salem Police Department because of her involvement, she and Abe separated. She then temporarily moved in with Jonah, but the two managed, not without effort, to fight the attraction between them. Jonah was expelled from the hospital where he had been studying medicine, but Lexie decided the family still needed a doctor in their ranks and took up medical studies herself. With Jonah's help, she quickly launched a new career goal. Eventually, Lexie's marriage was reconciled and became stronger than ever. She's now on the medical staff of University Hospital. Likewise, Jonah eventually was able to renew his medical studies.

Growing up, Lexie never knew her parents. She was brought up in an orphanage and was adopted by the Brookses, who later met a tragic end. Her aunt Frankie stepped in to support the young adult. It was quite a shock when Lexie decided to investigate her parentage and discovered that Aunt Frankie was really Celeste Perault, Stefano DiMera's longtime companion, and her mother. Soon after that shocker, Lexie also found out that Stefano was her father, a fact that had been kept from him too by Celeste. Lexie is often torn between her emotional need and inherent love for her father and her devotion and love for her husband, Abe.

The Kiriakis Mansion

13201 GLEN OAKS DRIVE

In another lakefront home in the wealthy part of Salem live Kate, Lucas, and Phillip, along with Henderson and the other servants. There is also room for other family members, who come and go at times.

In early 1995, Vivian tricked Victor into exchanging wedding vows. He thought it was a rehearsal for his wedding to Kate. After Kate was presumed dead when her plane went down over the ocean, Vivian spent a year comforting and seducing a mourning Victor.

Following Kate's one-year memorial, Vivian expected a night of passion, but Kate burst into Victor's bedroom and exposed all Vivian's lies and her role in Kate's absence. Vivian and her loyal servant, Ivan, were thrown out.

At a welcome-home party thrown by Victor, Kate was confused about why Austin and Carrie were apart and immediately became suspicious of Sami.

A few months later, while Victor and Kate watched TV in the family room, they heard Vivian announce she planned to sue for custody of Phillip. Later, when Victor confronted Vivian, he had a stroke.

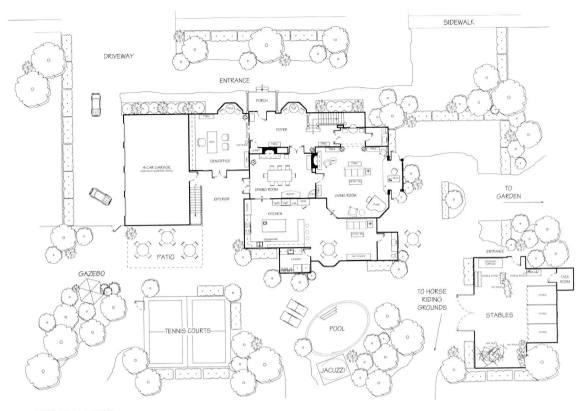

KIRIAKIS MANSION
MAIN LEVEL/GROUNDS

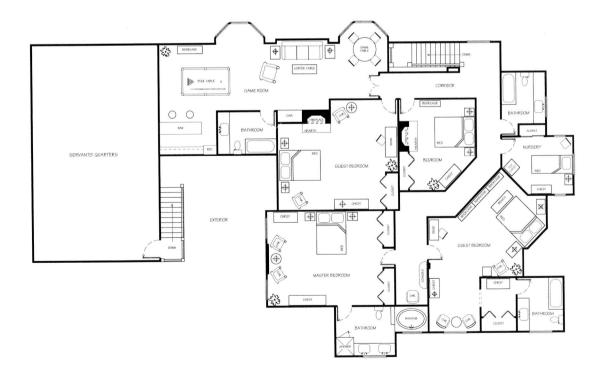

KIRIAKIS MANSION
SECOND LEVEL

Making a stand in the living room, Vivian claimed her rights as Victor's legal wife and kicked Kate out to stay at Marlena's penthouse. Soon Kate countered with her own rights as Phillip's mother and forced Vivian out.

With Nurse Lynn and Jamie's help, Kate exposed Sami's scheme: how she drugged Austin to get him into bed. Carrie hauled off with a slap that left Sami reeling.

Snooping in Kate's bedroom, Sami found incriminating information and photos that Kate had hidden in a secret drawer. The blackmail material served Sami well.

Kate's reunion with her family after returning from nearly a year on a fishing trawler was joyous, but filled with surprises. Not the least of which was her grandson Will. Kate was stunned to discover that Austin had not married Carrie and was immediately suspicious of Sami's sly innocence.

Sami shared some, but never all, of her manipulative secrets with Lucas, who had once been a real cohort and one-time fling. They even conspired to make it seem Carrie and Mike were more than just friends long before it turned out that way. They hoped Austin would then give up on Carrie and spend more time with Sami and baby Will. At the time, Lucas still had hopes that he could have a chance with Carrie.

In June 1996, while Kate and Sami were fighting over the blackmail material in front of Victor in the living room, and after he saw a photo of Kate as a call girl, he had another stroke.

Early in 1997, board members met at the Kiriakis mansion, where Victor was wheelchair bound. Most wanted to blackball Vivian from the company; but Kristen, who controls forty-nine percent and was being blackmailed by Vivian—who knew she had hired pregnant Susan to impersonate her—cast the deciding vote to keep her. She claimed she did it because as an Alamain, Vivian is related to her child with John.

By summer, Sami moved into the mansion using her own blackmail of Kate. She found out Kate had been a call girl and had hired Franco to break up Bo and Hope.

The den was the scene of Billie's heartbreak when Bo told her he could not deny his love for Hope after he realized Franco was never Hope's lover. Later, Hope and Billie had a confrontation and Billie told her that Bo made love to her in Rome.

Months later, pregnant Billie, threatening to leave Salem, almost fell from the staircase in her frenzied state. Bo managed to catch her, and she realized he cared enough that she could manipulate him to stay close to her. Later, a long way from Salem, she delivered a stillborn baby girl.

After Franco climbed through Sami's second-floor bedroom window, they made love. Lucas was aware of what was going on and manipulated Roman into going upstairs to say hello to his daughter, creating an embarrassing father-daughter moment.

Kate Roberts

While married to abusive Curtis Reed in the seventies, Kate had an affair with Dr. Bill Horton. Curtis found out about it, and her pregnancy. After beating her badly, he threw her out. Eventually, Curtis told her that their two children, Austin and Billie, were dead. Likewise, he told the children that their mother had first left them and then died.

Over the course of several decades, Kate established a new and very successful life for herself and her son Lucas, and she returned to Salem. Soon, Kate discovered that the journal she had written while in therapy with Dr. Marlena Evans during her first time in Salem had fallen into Jack Deveraux's hands. He submitted it to Titan Publishing as his own fiction, but Kate quickly locked it away. Still, at least one major part of her past came back to haunt her when presumed-dead Curtis reappeared. He tried to blackmail her and then turned up dead. Billie Reed was the prime suspect. During Billie's trial for murder, much came out about Curtis's links to Kate: their former marriage and the fact that Billie and Austin were her children, clearly very much alive too. The fact that Curtis had been alive when Kate married Victor Kiriakis invalidated that union, and made Kate a target for Vivian Alamain, who wanted Victor back.

Vivian made certain that all of Salem knew Lucas was Bill Horton's illegitimate son by Kate. Then, the child Kate planned to have with Victor through in vitro fertilization was cleverly stolen by Vivian, who carried their baby to term. As if that wasn't enough, after Vivian drugged the pilot's coffee, Kate's plane went down and she was presumed dead for about a year. All that time she was on a fishing boat.

Once back in Salem, Kate was caught up in a power struggle at Titan with Vivian and Sami, who each had blackmail material on Kate. She had to endure making Sami an executive at Titan and a welcomed houseguest at home, so she could be close to Will, her grandson.

Kate was devastated when Victor suffered a stroke and could not intervene in Titan business nor offer her a protective and caring shoulder. Meanwhile, Kate's children, Austin, Billie, and Lucas, each have had their love life problems. Kate, who once tried to help Billie land Bo as a husband, also found herself in a triangle with her daughter and Roman.

DID YOU KNOW:

She once stabbed Curtis with a butcher knife.

ᠻᡳᠯᢧ

As a high-price call girl she crossed paths with Stefano.

ᠻᡳᠯᢧ

Kate was thrown out by Curtis on Austin's third birthday.

Billie Reed

Billie came to Salem in 1993, a few months after her brother Austin arrived. In her first months in Salem, Billie lost a job because of her drug habit, became Carrie Brady's roommate, and would have fallen back into prostitution except for the intervention of Carrie's uncle Bo.

Billie and Bo quickly became romantically involved in spite of plenty of obstacles to their relationship, which included her formerly presumed-dead dad, Curtis, who kidnapped Stefano. Soon after, Curtis was found shot to death with Billie's gun. Bo stood by Billie during a trial that revealed: Curtis's incestuous relationship with Billie; Kate Roberts as her long-lost mother; and Stefano as the shooter who killed Curtis in self-defense.

On the night that Bo finally proposed marriage, a woman named Gina who looked incredibly like Hope, Bo's presumed-dead wife, was delivered cold, wet, and unconscious to their hotel room by Roman, who had saved her from Maison Blanche. She joined them back in Salem, but it was only after Bo wed Billie that

Gina regained her full memory and former life as Hope. The triangle was too difficult, and after a divorce, Billie left Salem and tended to European marketing for her Countess Wilhelmina cosmetic company.

Billie returned in 1996, shortly before Bo and Hope were to remarry. Her presence, and the manipulations of Franco Kelly, kept the wedding from taking place. She eventually rewed Bo in a marriage forced by drug dealer J. L. King, whom Bo was investigating in an undercover operation. The baby they conceived was stillborn, but Billie tried to hold on to Bo as her husband any way she could for a while.

However, when Bo's big brother, Roman, took off on another secret ISA mission, Billie stowed away and joined him. Unbeknownst to anyone else in Salem, Billie had already joined forces—physically and professionally—with the elder Brady when she stumbled upon him in Paris several years earlier. At that time they were each getting over broken relationships, with Marlena and Bo, respectively, just as they were again the second time.

⌘

Billie's letter to Bo when she was leaving Salem:

Bo,

You were not only my lover, you were my best friend in the whole world. And still, to this day, my heart belongs to you. For so long, I've tried to deny my love, to hide it, but it's too strong. No matter how hard I try, I couldn't stop loving you, needing you. I know that you love Hope; she's the first in your heart and always will be. That's why I'm writing this to you now. Because it seems wrong somehow to love someone so much and not let them know. Love is powerful, so I'm hoping even though you don't return my love, someday my love for you will touch your life for the better, if only from afar—like a ray of sunlight shining down to make a flower grow. Life will never be the way I hoped and dreamed it would be, but I pray it will be that way for you and Hope—filled with laughter and joy and much love for each other. And sometimes, a kind thought for someone who knows and loves you both so much.

All my love,

Billie

⌘

Lucas Roberts

When Lucas left military school and came to Salem, he arrived at a local concert, where he had an intimate interlude with the rock star. That set the tone for his often spontaneous and self-indulgent pursuits. This twenty-something executive in his mom's company is good-looking, spoiled, and a father to Will; Sami first thought the child was fathered by Lucas' half-brother, Austin, and never dreamed she had conceived by her one-night stand with Lucas.

Lucas would do anything in his power to get what he wants. But he was not able to have Carrie, the only woman he's fallen for so far. He's a single dad with a successful position at Titan and a bright future. Unfortunately, he also has a drinking problem. It led to a playtime accident with Will. That gave Sami the opportunity to exaggerate the situation and have Lucas investigated on child abuse charges for supposedly hitting Will, which was untrue. Lucas was even made to leave the mansion while Sami remained.

DID YOU KNOW:

He drives a red BMW convertible.

ᏆᎢᏆᎪ

Sami used to call him General because of his military school uniform.

Sami Brady

Because of their parents' many abductions, Sami and her twin brother, Eric, often spent large chunks of time with their maternal grandparents in Denver, Colorado. Sami returned to Salem in 1990 but didn't bring much attention to herself until she became infatuated with Carrie's boyfriend, Austin. Named for Samantha (Marlena's smart but unstable twin sister), Sami seems to share a few too many traits with her late aunt.

After happening upon her mom and John Black having an amorous encounter on a Titan conference table, her emotions ran amok. She became bulimic, lying, and vengeful.

Later, while she worked as a hospital volunteer and came upon family records, she altered blood-type and test results on a hospital computer to keep the true paternity of her half-sister, Belle, from dad Roman. It was John's baby. Sami went even further over the edge when she kidnapped the child and tried to have her adopted to rid the Brady household of the symbol of Marlena's affair.

She was raped by Alan Harris but suffered public humiliation when she brought him to court. Later, when he came after her with a gun, Sami found personal revenge by blowing away his manhood.

She drugged Carrie's beau, Austin Reed, to get him to make love to her. Then, on Carrie and Austin's wedding day, she turned up in Salem, pregnant with the groom's baby, putting an abrupt end to the ceremony. On Carrie and Austin's second wedding day, she wore a gown just like Carrie's and married Austin herself; the two needed to be "proper parents" by French standards to get baby Will back to Salem after he was kidnapped and then found in Paris.

After being hit by Austin's car, Sami nearly died, but when Austin played the music from their wedding and stayed at her side she returned from her near-death experience.

With the help of Lucas Roberts and Vivian Alamain, who each had their own agendas, Sami continued to scheme and connive to keep Austin tied to her and her son, Will—even after she discovered that Lucas, not Austin, was the baby's actual dad. Lucas, Austin, and the rest of Salem learned the truth on the day Sami was to wed Austin. Turning the tables, Carrie provided the hospital records that stopped this walk to the altar. After Carrie wed Austin within an hour of the rev-

DID YOU KNOW:

When Sami returned to Salem in early 1993, she broke into the house and set off a silent alarm that brought her dad running with gun in hand, so her first words were: "No, Dad!"

One of her favorite dolls is named Mollyanna.

While trying to fix a household appliance, an electric shock jolted the memory she had lost when Austin accidentally rammed her with his car.

elation, Sami showed up at the reception, uninvited of course, and snatched the wedding bouquet when Carrie tossed it to the single women in the room.

Since then, Sami was wooed and bedded by Franco, who needed an American wife in order to stay in the U.S. She blackmailed Kate into setting her up at the Kiriakis mansion so she'd be close to Will. Her blackmail also landed her a plum career position with Titan.

Upset by Lucas' drinking around Will and fearful that he would press for full custody of the child when she and Franco wed, Sami brought abuse charges against Lucas after a playtime accident put a bump on the boy's head.

Will Reed

His mother wanted Austin Reed so badly that she drugged Austin at a local bar and took him back to her apartment. She used Carrie's perfume and tricked him into making love. When Sami learned she was pregnant, she happily assumed it was Austin's child, conveniently forgetting that she had had a one-night stand with Lucas, Austin's half-brother, just two weeks earlier.

For a time, even before his actual birth, this sweet little boy became Sami's hold on Austin Reed. Sami and Austin eventually married only because, after his kidnap and rescue, he would have been put into foster care by French authorities if he didn't have "legal" parents.

Will spent the first few years of his life thinking Austin was his daddy. However, it turned out that Lucas was his biological father. The adjustment was not a smooth one, especially after Lucas dropped the boy during a game of airplane. Sami charged Lucas with child abuse, claiming the bump on Will's head came as a result of being hit by Lucas in a drunken haze.

Phillip Robert Kiriakis

The long-desired son of Victor Kiriakis and Kate Roberts, he was conceived in vitro and carried by scheming Vivian Alamain, who switched petri dishes in the fertility clinic and therefore managed to "steal" the couple's unborn baby.

Phillip was born just as Victor and Kate were to wed. Before the wedding vows were rescheduled, Vivian let it be known she really was wed to Victor (although he thought it was just a rehearsal for the ceremony with Kate). The stress of it all threw Victor into a stroke, so poor Phillip will never know his father. Victor is in a coma with no hope for improvement.

Placed in a nanny's care with only cousin Will to play with, Phillip will likely grow up to be another lonely rich kid.

The Deveraux House

1552 COPPERLANTERN DRIVE

Jack and Jennifer had been living in an apartment over Alice's Restaurant until Abby came along and they needed larger quarters. Jennifer's father, Bill, gave the couple the house he once owned. It's a Craftsman-style home, painted in pale colors. This particular house was built about 1915 and sits on a lot of approximately 120 by 90 feet.

After Jack found a large sum of money (a stash Billie was supposed to be holding for a past crime buddy) he went out and furnished the house for Jennifer. The decor is very much the same Craftsman style of the house.

The landscaping includes a lot of drought-tolerant and seasonal plants because both Jack and Jennifer like gardening. They buy plenty of annuals although there is more Mexican sage than roses throughout the garden. They enjoy relaxing on Sunset-style patio furniture.

In Abby's room, there are dolls from Jennifer's childhood as well as Abby's

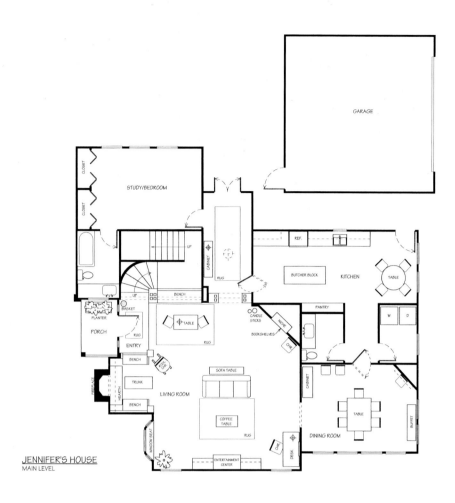

JENNIFER'S HOUSE
MAIN LEVEL

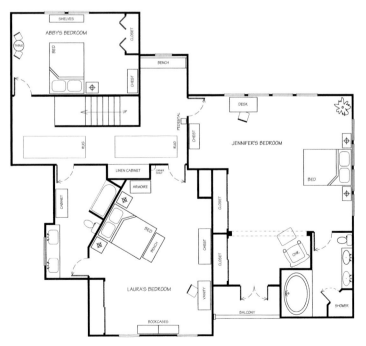

JENNIFER'S HOUSE
SECOND LEVEL

own. Jennifer is a collector too who likes to go to swap meets. Jack, a macho type, would like to collect cars. There's presently a three-car garage.

In spring 1996 Jennifer, fiancé Peter Blake, ex-husband Jack, daughter Abigail, and mom Laura lived at the house. Jack is also Laura's former short-term lover for whom she still has feelings—a fact Peter made sure Jennifer eventually found out.

The living room has been the primary point of confrontation in this house. After learning that Peter was involved with shady DiMera dealings and Jude St. Clair, and had played underhanded tricks on Laura to make her think she was losing her sanity again, Jennifer threw Peter out of the house.

Soon after, Peter returned with plans to kidnap Jennifer and Abby, but Jack intervened. In the tussle, Jack's gun went off and Peter was shot on the stairs. It seemed he was fatally shot when doctors couldn't save him at the hospital. Jack was arrested for murder.

Police came to the house several times to cart Jack away. Good-bye moments with his daughter were deeply moving.

Nurse Lynn was hired by Laura's visiting nurse when she was recuperating from the seemingly mysterious amnesia and delusions she was suffering. Laura saw Stefano with Lynn at the house and was almost hypnotized by Marlena, but Kristen stopped anything that would lead to the truth.

Mike, Jennifer's brother, moved into the house after returning from Israel, where his son, Jeremy, and ex-lover Robin still live. He wanted to be close to his mother to take care of her.

While Jack was in prison, and Peter secretly recuperating, Trent, aka Travis, bought neighbor Mr. Scranton's house to keep an eye on Jennifer and help Peter get her back. He even installed a security alarm system for her.

Christmas trees and special ornaments are a family tradition for all the Horton offspring. Fourth generation Abby got the hang of it!

After Travis kidnapped Jennifer from this house, the living room became a frequent gathering point of friends and family. Eventually, they rejoiced when Jack saved Jennifer from Travis and returned safely. However, they went undercover and on the lam to find Peter, but he found them. Luckily, after some intriguing circus stunts, Peter was captured and imprisoned.

When Laura became the prime suspect in the Blake house murder, old friends Abe and Roman had to execute a search warrant. They came through the house and went into Laura's things looking for evidence. Eventually, Laura was off the hook.

At present Laura and Mike share the house. Jack, Jennifer, and Abigail have gone to visit Jennifer's dad, Bill, for an undetermined length of time.

Laura Spencer Horton

Laura arrived in Salem in 1966 and became engaged to Bill Horton, but married his brother Mickey. Raped by Bill, she bore Mike, who was raised for many years by Mickey, who believed he was the boy's father. After a long-troubled marriage, Laura and Mickey divorced and she married Bill while pregnant with their daughter, Jennifer Rose. Bill had an extramarital affair with a woman named Kate. Still, he and Laura managed to repair their marriage. However, about a year later, Laura had a mental breakdown and Bill had her committed to a sanitarium, where she remained for nearly two decades.

In 1994, Laura and Vivian escaped from the corrupt institution that kept Laura overmedicated. The time away from Salem made it hard for her to cope, as did the presence of Kate Roberts and the brief visit of her now ex-husband, Bill. Luckily, she had the love and support of her children Jennifer and Mike, and many friends.

However, after she found out too much about Jennifer's fiancé Peter, he secretly tried to make it seem Laura was still psychotic and nearly succeeded.

Shaken by it all, Laura sought counseling at the Meadows, an unconventional center for emotional development. There, where everyone used pseudonyms, she unwittingly had a "therapeutic" affair with her former son-in-law Jack Deveraux, whom she had never before met. Only after Jack returned to Salem to see his daughter, Abigail, and tried to reconcile with his ex-wife, Jennifer, did Laura find

DID YOU KNOW:

Laura earned her degree in psychiatry at Johns Hopkins University.

ⓒ▩ⓥ

She gave birth to daughter Jennifer Rose in a farmhouse during a snowstorm.

ⓒ▩ⓥ

Her own mother had been institutionalized with mental illness; during her breakdown, Laura heard her mother telling her to kill herself. She tried.

Laura, no matter what trauma or trial she faces, is ferociously loyal to those she loves and courageous in all she does.

out "Clark" was Jack. They hid their former involvement from everyone, but eventually Jennifer learned of Laura and Jack's affair. She married Peter and rebuilt her relationship with her mother.

After Jack seemingly shot Peter dead, Laura again appeared psychotic, but it was because she had found out Peter was alive and Stefano had had a brain procedure performed on her to keep her quiet. When its effects waned, he succeeded in drugging her for a while. Eventually, she remembered everything and arrived at John and "Kristen's" wedding reception. When Marlena and the real Kristen were saved from the secret room, Laura was proved sane and freed of dangerous secrets.

Not much later, Laura's stability was again put to the test when it seemed Jennifer was killed in a car crash and Laura went after Kristen with a gun to avenge some of the DiMera deeds against her family. After Kristen was found dead in her swimming pool, Laura was a suspect. Eventually, Laura was cleared. Now, for the moment, Laura seems to be in a quieter state of mind without danger and intrigue surrounding her. She is, however, saddened that her daughter, Jennifer; Jack; and Abigail went off to South Africa to be with Jennifer's father, Bill, for a while.

Mike Horton

Raised by Mickey until his true paternity was revealed, Mike went through his teen years trying to find himself. After an early marriage to Margo Anderman, who died of leukemia, and a short career as a mechanic, he eventually turned to a medical career like his father, Bill; grandfather, Tom; and great-grandfather.

Mike had an affair with a woman named Robin Jacobs, and had a son, Jeremy, with her, but they never married because of their different religious beliefs. While Robin and Jeremy remain in Israel—where Mike also seems to have left some ghosts of poor judgment that cost many people their lives in a terrorist plot—he returned to Salem and worked at Salem University Medical Center. He eventually followed his grandfather's footsteps into the position of Chief of Staff.

For the first few years of his return, Mike had hardly any social life at all. He was immersed in the problems of his sister, Jennifer; her marriage; and her ex-husband's return. His mother's fragile mental-emotional state also took his time and energy. When he finally found love again he fell for Carrie, who soon after married her first love, Austin Reed. The two were childhood friends and the love they share could bring them both new pleasure and pain.

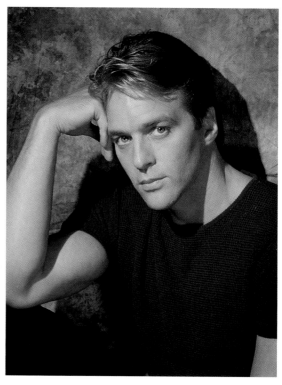

Mike's brooding sensuality found a lighthearted lift around Carrie, but he suffered plenty for his romantic love.

Jennifer Horton Deveraux Blake

The daughter of Laura and Bill Horton, Jennifer was raised by her dad and helpful relatives after her mother was institutionalized when Jennifer was just a youngster. She went through a rebellious stage as a teenager and was raped by Lawrence Alamain, whom she married under duress when a comparatively innocent ploy went awry. After many, many months of on-again-off-again courtship, Jennifer eventually married neurotic newspaperman Jack Deveraux, who had overcome a rather sordid past.

After their daughter, Abigail, became ill and was diagnosed with an illness caused by improper toxic waste disposal that Jack co-implemented, he left his family and divorced Jennifer, who went on to become a very successful television talk show host.

Jennifer found love again, this time with Peter Blake, the foster son of Stefano DiMera. Against her family's warnings, Jennifer jumped into the romance with this handsome, rich, and powerful man who treated her more like a woman than Jack had ever done. In many ways, Peter was a DiMera, but through Jennifer's love he made a number of attempts to change. However, he was raised to have his way; nothing could prevent his having Jennifer. Jennifer didn't find out for quite some time that the man she trusted tricked her mother to make her seem unstable and unreliable in her accusations against him.

When Jack returned to Salem, he was a much more secure and sensitive man. He wanted to win his wife and family back. Jennifer barely tolerated his constant presence (he still owned half the house and insisted on living there with Jennifer and Abby) and his assertion that Peter was not the good man she believed him to be.

Jennifer married Peter in 1995. She stood by her husband in spite of many situations that raised her doubts. However, Jennifer found out for herself that Jack had been right all along. Peter did love Jennifer, but was also deceptive and very much influenced by Stefano's upbringing. She learned how he tried to make Laura seem crazy. That was the final straw.

Jennifer had already filed for divorce when Jack shot Peter and apparently killed him on the night Peter attempted to kidnap Jennifer and Abigail from their beds. Jack went to prison and Peter secretly went into a long convalescence. While Jack was in prison, feisty Jennifer became a guard in disguise and joined Jack in trying to uncover prison system wrongs. In the process, she also became a target for Peter's hired man, Travis, who kidnapped her. Jack broke out of prison and managed to save Jennifer; after many dangerous twists and turns, Peter's duplicity was uncovered and he was sent to prison. Jack was cleared of murder and he and Jennifer spent time renewing their friendship with each other and as a family with Abigail.

D I D   Y O U   K N O W :

Jennifer knows how to hotwire cars and motorcycles, and can also get the coins out of pay phones and soda machines.

⟿

She learned how to skillfully play blackjack while in her college sorority.

⟿

Jennifer used to sing in a girls' chorus.

Jennifer and Jack's memorable songs

"Love Won't Let Me Wait" (at Hot Springs in 1993)

"Caught up in the Rapture"
(oh those strawberries! February 1993)

"Unchained Melody" (during dance-athon fundraiser)

"Perfect World" (on return from Aremid, 1996)

"Crazy for You"

"UnBreak My Heart"
(dance before Jack goes back to prison)

"How Do I Live" (Marlena getting ready for bed with John watching 7/21/97)

"Faithfully"
(instrumental—plays at Salem Club 11/9/96)

Jack and Jennifer had a roller-coaster courtship at the start and another tumultuous road back to each other in recent years.

Jack Deveraux

When Jack came to Salem in 1987 he had Hodgkin's disease. He became enamored of Kayla Brady, who loved Steve Johnson but married Jack when she felt rejected by Steve. They didn't consummate the relationship because of Jack's illness. After Jack was elected to the state assembly, insinuating photos of Kayla and Steve surfaced, and in a rage, Jack raped Kayla. After a fight with Steve in which Steve was injured, Jack donated a kidney to the man he discovered was really his brother. Jack and Kayla later divorced.

Jack was about to marry Melissa Anderson about a year later, but she distrusted his womanizing ways and left him at the altar. That wasn't Jack's only problem. He had plenty of family ghosts. Jack's adoptive father, corrupt politician Harper Deveraux, turned into a serial killer. Jack discovered his biological dad, Duke Johnson, was a wife-beating, daughter-raping misfit.

Jennifer Horton was an intern at *The Spectator* when Jack met her. Although they were attracted to each other, it took a clumsy start (he kidnapped her on the day she was to marry Emilio Ramirez) to admit his love. Still, their relationship was tumultuous. Jack married Eve and they divorced before Jack and Jennifer married in 1991.

After a wacky wedding, they set out on a honeymoon. Con artists swindled Jack out of his money and Jennifer used her trust fund to save Jack's interest in the newspaper. Jack was convinced he was going through a relapse of Hodgkin's disease when Jennifer announced she was pregnant, so he started to find her a more appropriate mate and sold the newspaper. Soon after, doctors convinced him he was in fine health and he became a police beat reporter. Later that year, Abigail was born.

Desperate and penniless, Jack tried many schemes to earn money, including retyping and submitting a manuscript he found in the house Bill Horton had given the couple as a wedding gift. When he found cash Billie Reed's crime buddy had stashed, he spent it, and the two tried a number of ways to replace it before Bo caught up with Tony Becker and made him leave town.

In 1992, Jack left town when Abigail's illness was traced to toxic waste

> **DID YOU KNOW:**
>
> Jack once proposed to Jennifer while wearing a Santa Claus outfit.
>
> ⁊⁊⁊
>
> The old Jack's idea of a romantic evening meant taking Jennifer to a baseball game.
>
> ⁊⁊⁊
>
> He was convinced he would die on a particular day and marked it on his calendar as The End.

dumping. He felt responsible for allowing his dad, Harper, to create the site years ago. He also filed for divorce from Jennifer while he was away, then tried to win her back when he popped up unannounced in Salem in 1994.

He was shocked to discover Jennifer had gone on with her life and found a new man. To try to win Jennifer back, he went to an emotional healing center, where he had a "therapeutic" affair with his ex-mother-in-law, whom he had never met because she had been institutionalized for almost twenty years.

He spent several years trying to prove Peter Blake was not the right man for Jennifer. Then, after she learned the dark truth about Peter and served him with divorce papers, Peter tried to kidnap her. Jack intervened and shot Peter. Jack was given a life sentence for murder but eventually escaped when Jennifer was kidnapped by Peter's henchman. Peter was alive and Jack first tracked down Travis, then Peter eventually revealed himself and was sent to prison, leaving Jack a free man able to renew his relationship with his ex-wife and daughter.

Abigail Johanna Deveraux

Seven-year-old daughter of Jennifer and Jack Deveraux, she is lavished with affection by great-grandmother Alice Horton and grandmother Laura. She recovered from aplastic anemia after she received a bone marrow transplant from Austin Reed. Although she didn't fully understand why she, her mom, and dad were living in motels, she did enjoy becoming a part of a traveling circus during the time Jack and Jennifer were alternately hiding from and trying to expose Peter. Their travels have taken them from Salem to the Grand Canyon and back; now the trio are off to South Africa.

The DiMera Mansion

430 LAKEVIEW DRIVE

Shane Donovan previously owned this house near the lake. He installed a large secret room that housed his ISA electronic equipment. Bo and Carly lived here for a short time after Shane left town, and eventually Stefano DiMera leased and remodeled it.

After their marriage, Tony DiMera bought the grand residence for himself and his wife Kristen. It's a large, opulent house with a lovely garden, pool, and the convenience of an elevator.

After Tony's death, the mysterious Woman in White, Kristen, John, and Marlena, fearful of kidnap by Stefano, lived together there.

In Marlena's guest bedroom Kristen found John's death row letter. Still unread by Marlena, it proclaimed John's love for Doc, so Kristen kept it from her.

In the living room, Marlena and Dr. Laura Horton often counseled the Woman in White, who through hypnosis and drugs revealed herself to be Kristen and Peter Blake's mother, Rachel, whom Stefano had pursued with obsession. He thought she died when he killed her husband.

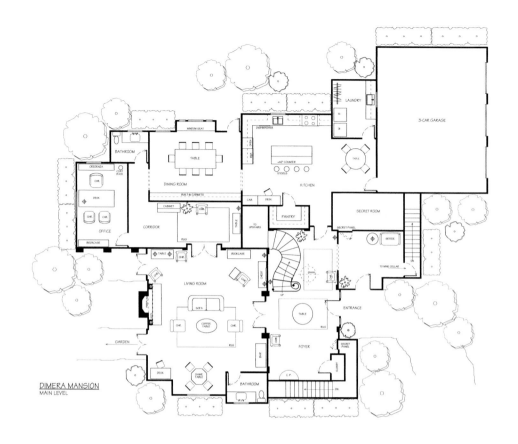

DIMERA MANSION
MAIN LEVEL

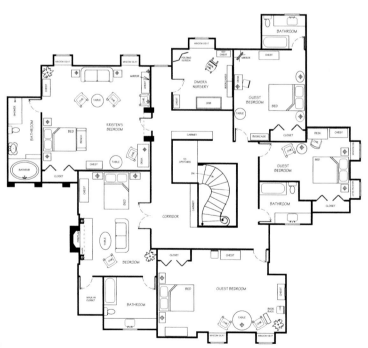

DIMERA MANSION
SECOND LEVEL

John too was treated with the same drug and remembered he had been Rachel Blake's confessor. That's why Stefano kidnapped John. While in a drug therapy state, John admitted to Laura that he loved Marlena more than Kristen, who overheard. Kristen then helped Stefano kidnap Marlena.

In another guest room, Kristen nearly poisoned Rachel before learning the woman was her mother. Both Kristen and Peter got an earful of stern motherly advice about the things each has done "for love" and she begged them to change their ways.

There is a secret room located off the foyer. It works on a complicated spring latch. When Stefano was attempting to kidnap Marlena, he tied up Rachel and hid her in this secret room. He then hijacked the plane and kidnapped Marlena, taking her to Paris.

In the wine cellar, John found a board game with uniquely carved pieces that intrigued him and eventually gave him the clues he needed to find Stefano's hiding place where he kept kidnapped Marlena.

Later in the year, after returning from their Paris adventure, Marlena stayed in the mansion with John and Kristen, who hid her miscarriage. She had the help of a pregnant look-alike, Susan Banks, who kept Kristen's doctors' appointments.

By June 1997, Kristen (actually Susan) had a baby. Things got even stranger in this mad mansion as identities shifted as easily as secret doors opened and closed. Susan came to stay as the baby's nanny and soon started studying Kristen's every move and mannerism. She was planning to take her baby back and win John too.

In the living room, Sister Mary Moira Banks, Susan's identical twin sister, sat talking to John and Kristen—who were unaware that it was really Susan.

Another secret room is located near the wine cellar. It is accessible through a door that opens when a faux bottle is given a firm-grasp turn. This room includes a few comforts: a bed, bath, television monitor, a food pantry, and an intercom. It could be watched on a small TV monitor Kristen usually carried with her.

Susan managed to lock Vivian and Ivan in this room, but Kristen let them out. Later Marlena discovered the touchstone she had given Susan in the DiMera living room, and figured out the baby scam. Kristen locked Marlena in the secret room and called Stefano to come and get her. Before he got there, Kristen herself was locked in the room with Marlena by Susan. It was the location of some knockdown confrontations between the two.

Furthermore, in a turnabout, Kristen and Marlena used that monitor to watch Susan (as Kristen) and clueless John's unique romantic romps in Kristen's bedroom. They also saw John proclaim his love for Marlena as he looked at her photograph in the living room. And they had a unique perspective on John and "Kristen's" Elvis-theme wedding at the mansion. They were finally rescued after Laura disrupted the reception and many truths were revealed.

Months later, after stopping Marlena from marrying John by delivering her still-alive ex-husband, Roman, Kristen had the foursome back in the mansion in

*Have yourself a merry DiMera Christmas! Complex and contradictory, Stefano
has always held fast to family loyalty and some traditional beliefs in spite of his
Machiavellian manipulations. In décor, opulence is always key.*

*Chess has always been the metaphor for Stefano's bigger moves that influence people's lives and
loves. John, both destroyed and re-created by Stefano, has often proved to be a worthy adversary in
Stefano's games.*

yet another charade. Using Roman's grave illness as a ploy, Kristen played the part of John's wife as Marlena nursed Roman back to health.

In the DiMera living room, Sami Brady proved she could lie even to her twin brother, Eric, without his knowing it. She used a metal file to inflict pain on herself and scramble the intuited message he got from her.

In Roman's guest room, he told Marlena he still loved her; he went into cardiac arrest but Marlena saved him.

In the garden, after Roman told Austin he was glad he was there for Sami, Austin proposed to Sami with no strings attached.

In the living room around the 1997 holidays, Kristen spiked Susan's eggnog and had her sign papers giving her all rights to baby Elvis.

In the foyer, a few days later, Kristen was confronted by another Banks—mobster-type Thomas—as well as Susan and Sister Mary Moira. Kristen showed them the custody papers and sent them on their way.

In early 1998, Peter, who was suffering jungle madness and looking for Jennifer and Jack, met with Stefano at the mansion.

For the next few months, the DiMera mansion was occupied by Stefano alone.

JONESY'S TOWN HOUSE

Actually among the DiMera holdings, this town house is in a nice part of town near parks and museums, on a street with a Washington, D.C., or San Francisco atmosphere. DiMera is a collector of all sorts of art and antiques, and many of his homes are storage places more than actual residences. Ornate, exquisite, marble-topped furniture in dark woods dominate. His taste tends toward Baroque Italian with a touch of art nouveau.

JONESY'S TOWN HOUSE

At the top of the entry staircase, the main doors open into a mudroom, then a foyer, before becoming the main part of the house, which is narrow and long. It has three levels (street level, main level, upstairs with two bedrooms).

Caretaker Jonesy became infatuated with Vivian, who he believed was a former lover, Flora Dora. He let Vivian believe he owned the town house and everything in it. This made him a perfect mark for the conniving Madame Vivian Alamain and her servant, Ivan.

The town house was the setting for a number of oddball antics, including a séance with Ivan as a gypsy psychic and Vivian dressed as Elvis; another ploy that entailed Vivian dressed as Bo Peep with her own sheep; a Halloween party to which Celeste was mystically drawn with Susan in tow; and a marriage ceremony with Ivan as the bogus priest.

While Jonesy and Vivian went to England, Kristen planned to meet Peter and give him the jungle madness cure. Instead, Celeste showed up, a struggle ensued, and Celeste was accidentally injected with the serum, which made her mad. When Stefano learned of the situation, he blasted Kristen and nearly disowned her, promising that she would never raise her son, Elvis.

When Stefano was hospitalized after a heart attack, Hope and Bo got into the basement to search for clues to her forgotten years. They recognized only one or two of many possibilities.

After Jonesy's honeymoon death, Vivian returned to Salem convinced that she owned the town house and everything in it. DiMera was curious about the situation and did not immediately set her straight.

Stefano entrusted Jonesy with his town house and all the art and antique treasures it held. Unfortunately, Jonesy fell for Vivian and willed her "his" possessions before he died. Now Stefano is working hard to secretly regain his property and possessions without revealing his connection to Jonesy.

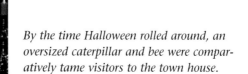

By the time Halloween rolled around, an oversized caterpillar and bee were comparatively tame visitors to the town house.

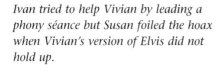

Ivan tried to help Vivian by leading a phony séance but Susan foiled the hoax when Vivian's version of Elvis did not hold up.

OTHER DIMERA REAL ESTATE IN SALEM

Another DiMera home in Salem is the original Chandler Mansion. It has a secret passage that leads to Doug's Place (formerly Sergio's) and a secret room where Julie and Doug Williams discovered DiMera's research on Salem, including aerial shots of the town, secret photos of residents, family trees, and maps. This is where Renée Dumonde (Stefano's daughter), David Banning, Tony DiMera, and Anna Brady DiMera lived together after Stefano "died," with explicit instructions about how his will would eventually be divided. This property was also called Marshall Manor after Alex Marshall inherited the home when his bride, Renée, was murdered.

At Ridgecrest, on the low-lying mountains adjacent to Salem, Stefano had a compound. It was where he kept Marlena and Liz hostage for a very short time in the early eighties.

DiMera has several warehouses. In one, John found those high-tech goggles that let him peek into Marlena's Paris prison. When Stefano realized John was on to them, his henchman planted a bomb that could have killed both John and Kristen. Luckily, it didn't.

Stefano DiMera

Stefano has lived up to his Phoenix nickname time and time again, as he's escaped capture, death (including being shot by Marlena, thrown from a penthouse by a demon, struck by lightning, and blown up), and justice since he first set foot in Salem in 1982. The Brady family became his target of obsession after Roman caused problems for his criminal enterprises in the early eighties. He's also responsible for John Black's lack of a complete personal history; while Hope Brady was held captive at Maison Blanche she too had a major memory lapse. Stefano erased most, if not all, of Laura Horton's memory too, and has managed to manipulate Vivian by an implanted gizmo in her molar. Stefano makes certain he always has control!

Only several years ago Stefano learned that Lexie Carver (ironically, the wife of Salem's Chief of Police Abe Carver) is his daughter by his longtime confidante, Celeste. Last year he lost his son, Tony DiMera, who was perhaps the closest person to him ever. Stefano saved his foster son, Peter Blake's, life and stole him away from Salem after making it appear Jack Deveraux killed Peter. When Peter returned to Salem and revealed himself, he was captured and jailed. Stefano has made certain Peter is comfortable in a prison of choice at some unknown locale. He helped Kristen Blake con John Black into thinking she was having his baby when a pregnant look-alike did the job for her.

Stefano's list of mistresses and children will never be complete. It seemed his tenacious fascination with Dr. Marlena Evans would never wane either. He has kidnapped her many times but has yet to convince her to come to him willingly. He came closest when he made nightly secret visits to her bedroom and led her away on hypnotic trips to a romantic world of his making. Unfortunately, that experience opened Marlena to possession by Satan. Stefano suffered several broken bones and his own amnesia after being tossed out a window by one of her resident demons. After her exorcism, Marlena nursed him back to health, but a lightning bolt jolted his memory, and evil ways, back.

Stefano is the major and most consistent source of problems for everyone in Salem, even though he's managed to become a free, if not always welcomed, citizen of Salem. He managed that by finding a cure for dying Roman. After Kristen's apparent death, he inherited forty-nine percent of Titan Publishing. Stefano is a bigger and more present threat to many more people in Salem than ever before.

Celeste Perault

This exotic woman first showed up at the DiMera estate in New Orleans, Maison Blanche, in 1994. Celeste was the keeper of plenty of secrets and held ample resentment against Marlena for being the object of Stefano's obsession.

Once back in Salem, Celeste maintained her silence and loyalty to Stefano. She was Stefano's longtime confidante and former mistress. She was also the woman Lexie Carver knew as Aunt Frankie. However, Celeste turned out to be Lexie's mother, who hid that fact, and the identity of Lexie's father, Stefano, from everyone, including DiMera himself. When Lexie investigated her parentage and the truth became known, Celeste made a choice between Lexie and Stefano. Although he will always have influence over Celeste, her main concern is always to protect her daughter, even from Stefano if she must.

While noted for her psychic abilities and high-fashion sophistication, Celeste joined forces with Vivian to test her business acumen at Alamain's company, which is in competition with Titan, owned by Kate Roberts and forty-nine-percent stockholder, Stefano.

Even while out of sight and far away, Celeste used the wealth and savvy she learned from Stefano to protect and care for her daughter, Lexie, who was adopted as an infant.

The Alamain Mansion

4930 CHESTNUT STREET

This rather European-looking mansion was the Salem home to Lawrence Alamain, who had indeed been born in Europe and raised in a number of far-away places. He came to Salem in 1990 when he tried, in vain, through Jencon Oil to establish a refinery that would have upset the town's aesthetic and ecological values.

The mansion was also the site of Emilio Ramirez's death in 1990 when he fell out a window during a heated argument with Melissa. It had also been the film location for a horror movie, which Roman had shut down after Nick's apparent murder.

Vivian, Lawrence's aunt, arrived in Salem in time to save him from an intruder threatening Lawrence at the Alamain mansion. Afterward, Lawrence casually greeted his aunt who had arrived without announcement.

In 1992, after discovering that Nikki Alamain was Carly and Lawrence's son and not Vivian's foster son, Lisanne Gardner threatened to blackmail Vivian. Nikki overheard the sounds of confrontation and came in, giving Lisanne a sud-

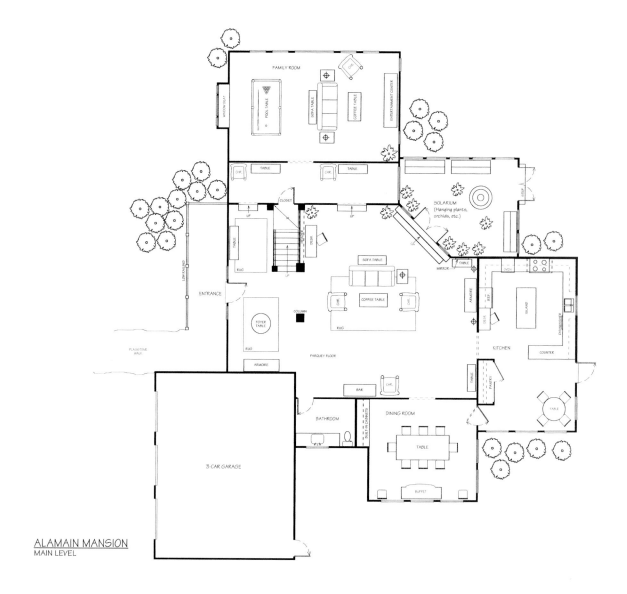

ALAMAIN MANSION
MAIN LEVEL

den push that sent her tumbling. Her head hit a stone cat and she was dead. To protect Nikki, however, there were plenty of hijinks to make Lisanne's death look like a car accident.

In a bedroom at the Alamain house, Lawrence almost bedded Carrie, but John, with gun in hand, interrupted the would-be moment.

After John was verified as Lawrence's brother, there were many arguments between Vivian and Lawrence over the money she swindled from Forrest Alamain's trust that now belonged to John.

In 1993, Carly secretly recuperated in a guest room at the mansion after being rescued from her grave, where she had been buried alive by Vivian.

A year later, Vivian and Laura recuperated from their harrowing experiences at the sanitarium.

In 1995, Vivian burned down the Alamain house.

Vivian Alamain

Vivian Alamain lost most of her wealth soon after landing in Salem and discovering that her nephew, Forrest Alamain, had not died. He was, in fact, John Black and the rightful heir to Alamain money. John was shocked to discover that Vivian swindled him out of Forrest's portion of his father, Leopold's, inheritance. With Victor Kiriakis' help, John got his share of the fortune. Vivian received an allowance from Lawrence and focused her romantic interests on the richest man in Salem, Victor.

Her stronger emotional attachment was to her foster son, Nikki. In truth, the boy was really the son of Lawrence and Dr. Carly Manning, who had both been told the baby died. When Lawrence learned his son was still alive, Vivian was fearful she would lose Nikki, and kidnapped him. Nikki was found, but Vivian, diagnosed with a fatal heart problem, tried to jump from the hospital roof, making it look as if Carly pushed her. Vivian survived, but while in the hospital, she started taking mysterious Asian herbs. It cured her heart but made her insane. She killed several of Carly's patients before Carly discovered her in the act. Vivian then

injected Carly with a potion that made her appear dead, and managed to bury Carly alive and even taunted her from above ground about Nikki. Luckily, Vivian had a flash of sanity and Lawrence rescued Carly. Lawrence, Carly, and Nikki left Salem for Europe.

Vivian was admitted to a sanitarium, where she discovered Laura Horton, a link to Kate Roberts' secret past. She also learned of illegal operations there and nearly underwent a lobotomy before the place caught fire. She and Laura escaped with Ivan's help.

Back in Salem, Vivian's shenanigans included: revealing Kate was still married when she married Victor, and that Lucas Roberts' father was Bill Horton; marrying Victor herself, although the groom thought it was a wedding rehearsal; stealing Victor and Kate's in vitro embryo and having it implanted in her own womb; delivering their son, Phillip; inadvertently causing Kate's plane to crash and thereby keeping Kate out of Salem for a year; and sending Victor into a stroke when she told him she was suing for custody of Phillip.

After being ousted from the Kiriakis mansion and using the last of her funds to get out of jail after Kristen's hijinks collapsed, Vivian was virtually penniless for many months before marrying Jonesy and inheriting a town house laden with riches. Little did she know she also inherited trouble. Everything actually belonged to Stefano. Meanwhile, Vivian started a new company that she hopes will eventually destroy Kate and Titan.

Ivan Marais

Ivan was totally devoted to Vivian Alamain long before she brought him to Salem in 1992. Knowing neither fear nor humiliation, this servant/companion is loyal beyond reason to his Madame. When Vivian accidentally contributed to Lisanne Gardner's death, Ivan toted the body away, created a car crash, and arranged for cremation. He helped Madame obtain the Asian herbs that drove her to murdering hospital patients. Of course, he never gave her up to authorities. Ivan stood by her side as she tortured Carly, buried alive. He helped Vivian even while she was in the sanitarium, taking a job as an orderly to be close to her. Luckily, he saved her from being lobotomized, or burned in the institution's fire. He stood by her after she lost her wealth. Ivan has aided every plot Vivian has created, although with periodic reservations. He dressed as a woman on more than one occasion; he donated his sperm and helped Vivian switch petri dishes to end up pregnant with the Kiriakis baby. He's been in jail with her, proposed to her, and suffers her abuse. After she was thrown out of the Kiriakis mansion for the final time and used the last of her money to get out of jail, Ivan never left her. He found odd jobs and helped Vivian ensnare Jonesy's affections and stood by as she married him. Whatever is ahead for Ivan, it will always be linked to Vivian's fate.

Roman and Marlena's House

334 SYCAMORE STREET

This is the house where Roman lived with Marlena. Later, when John was thought to be Roman, he lived here too.

Returning to Salem after his divorce and another resurrection from the grave, Roman went head to head with John over Marlena. He even bought back the house they once lived in together as a special gift. They never lived in it again, because within a few months it became clear that he could never make Marlena choose between John and him, and bowed out of the romance race.

It was bombed in 1986, and Marlena was believed to have died. Clearly, she didn't. The following year, Carrie hid her friend Jonah Carver in the house when he briefly ran away from home as a prank.

A decade later, after Roman and Marlena separated and then divorced, Marlena moved into the penthouse John bought for her. Shortly after, Roman left town. Carrie had already found an apartment; Sami, too, moved into an apartment of her own.

The house was sold, but Roman bought it back when he thought that he and Marlena would be reunited after his health returned following his mysterious ISA mission that had left friends and family thinking he was dead.

Roman Brady

A police officer and ISA agent, Roman was born and raised in Salem. He became the unlucky focus of Stefano DiMera's hatred after interfering with the international crime boss's illegal Salem activities. Stefano also became intrigued with Roman's wife, Marlena. Roman was once held captive by Stefano but presumed dead by his family and friends. When he apparently returned to Salem in 1986, he found his wife with another "Roman" but immediately set that record straight. However, when Marlena had a baby by John Black in 1991, Roman divorced her and left town. He went off on a secret crime-fighting mission and the next thing his friends and family were told in 1997 was that he was killed. His closed casket was sent back to Salem and there was a memorial service and burial. However, Roman turned out to be alive and was returned, quite ill, by Kristen Blake just in time to stop the wedding between Marlena and John. After months of push and pull passion, the triangle finally was broken when Roman stepped aside for John and Marlena to pursue their soul-mate relationship. It wasn't too long before Roman was involved in other romances of his own.

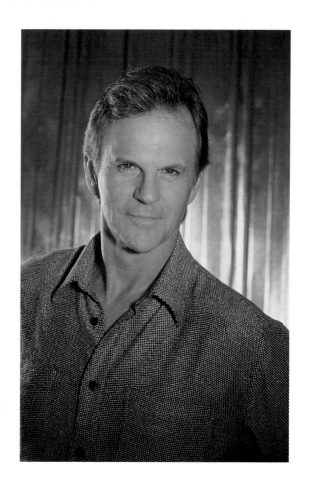

DID YOU KNOW:

Roman met his first wife, Anna Fredericks, in a library; after she and Roman divorced, she married Tony DiMera.

☙

Roman makes a great chili dog but is also known for his hamburgers when he barbecues at Brady–Horton parties.

☙

His favorite ice cream is butter pecan.

Roman Brady was the love of Marlena's life until he was abducted by Stefano and presumed dead. Although they had a good life together after his return, Roman and Marlena divorced after she gave birth to John's baby, Belle.

Mickey and Maggie Horton's House

415 ARDMOUR

A very traditional and comfortable home with lots of wood and stone, it is decorated in a warm contemporary American style. It's a fairly large home with three bedrooms. Maggie decorates in dark wood and Queen Anne–style furniture, and there are pieces from the Alice and late Tom Horton house too.

Prior to this, Mickey and Maggie lived on her Simmons family farm. Then the couple had a town house before buying this house near the lake.

Salem Newcomers

Craig Wesley

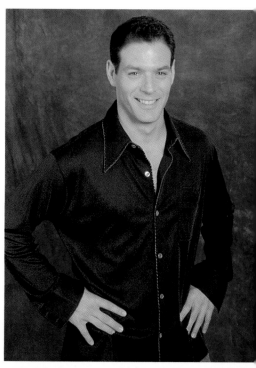

This old medical school chum of Mike Horton always had an edgy rival attitude. That was clear when they crossed paths after many years at a medical convention in Los Angeles months before good-looking Craig settled in Salem. Within weeks of his arrival in Mike's hometown, Craig made it clear the rivalry had reached new levels. He wanted the Chief of Staff position Mike was also hoping to land. Even Craig's dirty dealing and manipulations, however, could not get the upper hand. Mike won the Chief of Staff job. That only made Craig more determined to cause Mike trouble, and the hospital has become a prime locale for sneaky intrigue.

Nancy Wesley

Clearly raised with money and with a penchant for getting her own way, Craig's wife is just as conniving as her husband. Since she's always had whatever she's wanted, Nancy is now focused on getting for Craig whatever it is he wants. Even though the duo were unsuccessful in their scheming during the Chief of Staff campaign, this couple has new plots to cause Mike trouble. Nancy is convinced that, eventually, Craig will head Salem University Hospital, no matter what!

Nicole Walker

This tall, attractive young woman first made a living as a waitress at the Java Café where she caught the eye of Eric Brady. Soon after, Eric's sister Sami was put in charge of *Bella* magazine's "New Faces" campaign. He was hired as a photographer and Nicole became a top model. Her romantic relationship with Eric suffered when her former flame, Jay, came to Salem and tried to rape her. Discovering Nicole's lies took Eric aback. Their relationship will never be quite the same, but Nicole has her sights fixed on success and happiness and that includes Eric.

Taylor Raines

She first popped up in Salem as a cleaning girl in the Titan building. Immediately, she noticed handsome Eric Brady working late at the *Bella* photo studio. Before long it became clear that Taylor had another connection at *Bella*, and a rival. Taylor and *Bella* model Nicole are sisters and Eric will find himself in the middle of a romantic triangle, and more.

Ali McIntyre

This pretty, young nurse is quite ambitious. She has her eyes on a career and a relationship with the hospital's Chief of Staff, Dr. Mike Horton. She doesn't realize, however, that she's being used by Nancy and Craig Wesley to get Dr. Horton ousted from the position Dr. Wesley has always wanted. Caught in Mike's arms more than once by Carrie, she also provokes Carrie's jealousy. Ali could be in the middle of her own personal trauma center before too long.

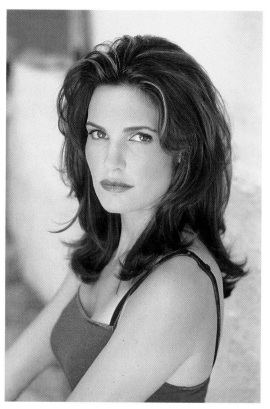

Lili Faversham

This delightful, rich woman was first introduced while living in Lugano, Switzerland. After a few months it became clear that she has some interesting ties to people in Salem, even if she had not known them by their real names. She was certain that Hope was a "Princess" Gina; also, she didn't realize that the two people she knew as "Jesse Bob" and "Ruth Ann," were, in fact, Roman and Billie. She's also met Stefano. After tripping about Europe with Hope for a little while, Ms. Faversham arrived in Salem to discover and uncover several other relationships.

Greta

As the key to the secrets of John's and Hope's missing years, Greta was innocently caught up in Ernesto's and Stefano's plot many years ago. When Hope was apparently killed in an exploding cage over acid, it was Greta, the magician's assistant, who took the fall and bears the scars of the illusion that went wrong. Both Hope and Greta were whisked away by Stefano. Now, many years later, Greta has been found hiding in the bayou, protected by Wayne and Earl, and their mom, Erlene. This Swamp Girl and Bo have developed a close relationship. Slowly, he's pulled her out of her physical and emotional trauma and brought her to Salem to face her past enemy, Stefano; discover an old friend, John; and to make new ones.

Part Three

Salem Business District

Shopping and Other Businesses

Salem Place

Since it opened in July of 1992, this charming and convenient mall with shops, eateries, and a cinema has become a crossroads and popular meeting place for Salem residents.

The entire mall is decorated seasonally and is the site for the huge Salem Christmas tree each year. When it was set ablaze in early December of 1994, it was among the first casualties of the Salem Desecrator. At the 1996 lighting, Abby and every other Salem resident present prayed for Abby's grandmother Laura to be found. She was found, just before Christmas, in an adjacent park.

In fall of 1996, Jennifer saw Peter chatting with Daniel Scott. Later, when she could talk to Daniel alone, she pretended to know everything Peter had been

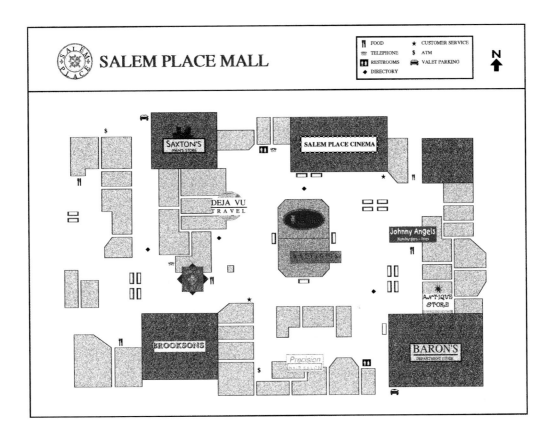

secretly doing. When Daniel fell for the ploy, he told her details of everything Peter had done, including tricking her mother, Laura.

It was in the mall in late 1997 that Marlena and Celeste figured out that Stefano was baby Elvis's father. When they confronted him there, he laughed off the thought.

After Laura confronted Kristen about knowing that Peter was still alive, Laura dropped her prescription pills, placiden, which Kristen then pocketed. They would later become evidence that police used in trying to link Laura to the death of Kristen in the Blake house pool.

Ballistix

Carrie worked in this upscale women's clothing shop for a short time in 1992.

On the first day of the mall's opening, a band played outside and a good-looking guitar player caught Carrie's and most other girls' attention. Later, he came into the shop to buy a shirt. Because all the dressing rooms were occupied, he quickly took off his own shirt and tried on the new one in the middle of the store, flustering Carrie even more. Later, it turned out that the same fellow lived in an apartment next door to Carrie's. She had enjoyed the piano music coming from that apartment even before she met Austin.

Most of Salem's women pick up a piece of wardrobe here at one time or another.

Salem Hair Design

Located next to Ballistix, it's a popular full-service beauty salon.

In 1993, after Jennifer started cutting her hair herself, she went to this shop to have it correctly cut and styled.

Java Café

This is a trendy shop with plenty of outside stools and seating, a great place to meet, gossip, and weave intrigue, all in such a harmless atmosphere!

Nicole was a waitress here when Eric first spotted her and became fascinated. She quit her job after starting to model for Sami's *Bella* magazine campaign.

Stefano and Lexie were brought together in worry over her mother Celeste when she was missing and wandering about with a case of jungle madness. They searched everywhere, including Salem Place.

Nicole was a waitress at the Java Café when she caught Eric's eye.

Johnny Angel's

This burger-fries-shake kind of fast food stand has high counters and stools for shoppers in a hurry, or Salem residents who want to watch the crowds pass by. Like Java Café, it's a great place to gather gossip and stir secret plans.

Salem Cinema

The local theater features current movies and periodically holds film festivals of one kind or another.

Several years ago, there was a Laurel and Hardy festival. It also rents out for private screenings like the one John offered Marlena, an exclusive movie date for just the two of them in fifties style. The movie was *Grease*, and while John wore his black leather jacket, Marlena wore a poodle skirt and had her hair in a ponytail.

The cinema also provided Franco with an alibi during his first few months in Salem when he was accused of attacking Jill.

John and Marlena's movie date

"Back in My Arms Again"

"My Girl"

"Marvin, Marvin"

"Ain't Nothing Like the Real Thing"

"Hopelessly Devoted to You"

"Grease"

Saxton's

This conservative men's clothing store specializes in a wide size range of men's suits and coordinates.

Steve, Julie Williams' brother, worked here very briefly in 1989 before he left Salem for the last time.

Simone's

This women's boutique specializes in evening wear. It's where both Hope and Billie bought dresses for a special date with Bo.

The Gift Box

Bo and Hope bought their original wedding rings at this fair-priced jewelry store.

A.N.O. Electronics

When this waterfront retail store was robbed, Jonah and Lexie captured the thief. It was during the time Jonah was the vigilante called the Pacifier and Lexie was still on the police force, trying to keep him safe.

Book Ends

This small bookstore is located on the riverfront shopping district.

Baron's Department Store

One of Salem's larger department stores, Billie and Bo were once trapped inside overnight.

Bartlett's Department Store

One of the oldest department stores in Salem, it's not as large as Baron's. Julie Olson stole a fur piece from the store when she was a teenager.

Chez Julie

This was an antique shop that Julie opened. Her brother, Steven, helped her run it for a while, but he got involved in some shady dealings and eventually left town.

Anderson Manufacturing

For a time in the 1970s, this was one of Salem's largest corporations, a commercial construction and industrial development company owned by Bob Anderson.

A & J Construction

This was a building company started by Adrienne and Justin. When it failed, they moved to Dallas.

Anna DiMera Designs

This signature label fashion company was popular in the mid-1980s.

Jencon Oil

Owned by Lawrence Alamain, this company was involved in oil drilling on the Salem Riverfront.

Ecosystems

This ecology-minded company was founded by Isabella Toscano Black not long before she died. John, Victor, Vivian, Lawrence, and Carly were once all on the board together and held their meetings at the Alamain mansion.

Countess Wilhelmina Cosmetics

This is the business that Billie Reed won in a poker game. Starting out with the help of one chemist, Billie took her cosmetic line from a small booth in Salem Place to a large company that she now runs through Titan Enterprises, which is the overall corporation to Titan Publishing and related ventures. Products are distributed internationally through boutiques and department stores.

Alamain International

When Vivian believed that she had rightly inherited a fortune from Jonesy, she set about liquidating the assets into cash. However, she did want to cause her rival Kate some grief, so she started this company with offices in the Titan building, and in direct competition with Titan Publishing.

Marlena and her twins Eric and Sami shared Christmas shopping.

Spas and Gyms

The Body Connection

This health club was once owned and operated by Chris Kositchek. Megan Hathaway tried to murder Hope here by rigging a hot tub to electrocute her. Instead Megan was accidentally killed by Larry Welch. The club was later bought by Tod Chandler.

Titan Health Club

This full-service facility is part of the Titan building complex. Located in the basement, its grand opening was held on July 14, 1994. It is open to the public, although it's used often by hardworking Titan employees. Alan, who raped Sami, worked here for a short time. Austin always liked to work out with the punching bag, and that gave Franco the idea to bring his coach around to entice Austin back into the ring.

The Spa

Another facility in town, this one offers day-of-beauty packages. It's where Marlena, Laura, and Lexie went for a day of pampering and relaxation before Marlena's wedding to John. That wedding was interrupted by Kristen's delivering a critically ill Roman.

At this spa, Stefano disguised himself as a masseur and planned to kidnap Marlena. However, Lexie recognized him and he got away.

When Laura was enjoying a birthday massage, with Maggie and Celeste along for company, Peter tried the same tactic and disguised himself as the massage therapist. He nearly strangled Laura during a bout of jungle madness.

Titan's gym was the most popular gym in town for a while. It's still convenient for the many Salem residents working in the high-rise tower.

John and Lucas are consistent in their workouts.

Across town a professional sports gym suits Austin and other boxers.

Banks

Salem Union Bank

Along with other nationwide banks, this one is Salem's own local financial institution.

Salem Federal Savings and Loan

Another locally founded bank, this one gave Diana Colville the loan to start *The Spectator*.

The Docks

Over the years, the dock areas and piers on the river have been the sites for romantic moments, heartbreaking conversations, disappearances into misty fog, and loving reunions. There have been drug busts, shoot-outs, and secret meetings. There has been action of all sorts.

In recent times, there have been heroic moments. When Will and his stroller were accidentally knocked into the river, Carrie immediately dove in to rescue the child. Austin, hearing the commotion, dove in following them both. At the hospital later, bloodwork was done on Will as part of his postaccident exam. Later, when records were sent to Sami, she noticed that Will's blood type was not as expected and finally realized that Lucas, not Austin, was the boy's father. She kept that piece of information to herself.

Franco, though less self-sacrificing, also helped Shawn out of a tight spot here too. The move ingratiated him to the Brady family, something he needed in order to be accepted by more people in Salem.

Hope found eccentric Benny along the docks. Although it eventually led to his demise, the information he gathered on his shortwave radio became a link to Stefano, who was pretending to be dead at the time.

In early 1997, Bo met with Billie and told her that although he read her good-

When Austin asked Carrie to pick up baby Will while he ran errands, no one suspected that a cargo accident would send the baby's stroller into the river, with Carrie jumping in after, followed by Austin.

The docks along the riverfront stretch from industrial and warehouse areas to dockside parks and walkways.

bye note, he didn't want her to leave town. Hope was nearby behind some crates, and overheard Bo say he loves Billie, but didn't wait to hear the key phrase, "as a friend."

It was at the dock area that J. L. King set Bo up. Bo nearly busted a guy who claimed he'd just lost everything in a poker game, then dropped a bag full of money as he left. After Bo picked it up, J. L. King used a videotape as blackmail, indicating Bo was a dirty cop.

Bo and Abe would meet under the pier to discuss the undercover drug operation that kept Bo apart from Hope and close to Billie when she refused the witness protection program.

At the pier Hope saw Billie talking to Max and assumed she was scoring some drugs. Later, a larger drug deal was called off because of Hope's inopportune arrival.

At the end of 1997, John stopped Kristen from killing herself as she prepared to jump into freezing Salem River.

After what appeared to be Kristen's death by drowning in her pool, Laura threw her gunpowder-stained gloves into the river. Ironically, a fisherman just happened to pull one up when a particularly savvy police officer was close by and noticed, taking the glove back to the station as possible evidence.

The pier area is also the setting for the annual Thanksgiving feeding of the homeless.

Media

WGTB-TV

This TV station was previously WATB, where Jennifer worked as a reporter along with Madeline. In a short time, she anchored a talk show. After Jack left town, Jennifer cohosted some segments with Austin.

Salem Today

A magazine around since the mid-1980s, *Salem Today* contained an advice-to-the-lovelorn column written by Eugene Bradford under the pseudonym Bettina Lovecraft.

Titan Publishing

14 SALEM CIRCLE

This high-rise building contains several magazines, a cosmetics company, a restaurant, spa, gym, and other facilities.

Bella Magazine, founded by Victor Kiriakis in 1992 and named after his daughter, Isabella, is a modern fashion publication.

After acid scars on her face were erased, Carrie was featured on the magazine cover as the winning "Face of the Nineties." Later, in 1996, Carrie and Austin were both featured as models. She now has a position in the public relations department. Hope and Franco, models for Countess Wilhelmina's "Secrets" perfume, have been featured in ad campaigns in *Bella*.

Titan operates several photo labs and studios within its corporate building. While Kate Roberts owned fifty-one percent of the enterprise, and the building from top to bottom, Kate assigned Vivian an office: Sub-Basement 140.

There has been plenty of drama in the building. During a blackout, enemies Kate and Vivian were trapped for hours in an elevator while Kate's sons, Lucas and Austin, manually worked to move the elevator car to a position where the doors could be forcibly opened.

Franco and Hope were also trapped in a malfunctioning elevator car. At the time, Franco was suspected of attacking women in Salem. The situation was

Titan Publishing produces several other periodicals in addition to Bella, *for which it is most noted. In another division, Countess Wilhelmina perfumes and cosmetics broaden the company's portfolio.*

nerve-racking for Hope, but Franco soothed her with tales of his childhood. He just thought she was claustrophobic.

John and Marlena had a secret encounter on a boardroom table in a conference room adjacent to a party taking place. Unfortunately, Marlena's daughter, Sami, saw the duo. The impact of the scene caused Sami deep emotional trauma.

At quite another time, Sami and Lucas made love in the photo gallery. Austin walked in and mistakenly thought Lucas was with Carrie.

While Carrie was delivering an important presentation, Sami once barged into the conference room and accused Carrie of trying to steal her husband. Carrie's potential clients and other Titan VIPs walked out on her.

To appease Sami, Kate hired her, then was pressured by Sami's blackmail into promoting her.

Sami and Roman had an interesting father-daughter talk in her office after she bemoaned the fact that she didn't know what love really was. Roman pointed out that she could tell if a man really loved her by the way he treated her. Franco overheard the exchange and was delighted to have come across a means to manipulate Sami to his advantage. Soon after, Franco suggested Sami develop a more professional look and treated her to a complete makeover, hand-holding her at every step of the way.

Sami manipulated Kate into allowing her to launch a New Faces campaign. She then hired Eric as a staff photographer. Former Java Café waitress Nicole became Sami's first find. Soon after, Eric and Nicole were on the way to a bumpy romance.

Salem Chronicle

3113 CATALINA AVENUE

This publication is among the oldest in Salem. It's in a traditional format and the only real competition to *The Spectator*.

The Spectator

Tabloid in format but not content, this newspaper was founded and run by Philip Colville, but he lost interest after several years. It was relaunched and rejuvenated by his daughter, Diana, in 1988. She ran it with Calliope for several months until Jack bought fifty-one percent of the newspaper. Then he and Vern Scofield ran it together.

Jennifer was working here as an intern when she met Jack and they started

One-upmanship is a game Sami loves to tackle. After half-sister Carrie landed a powerful position at Titan, Sami set her sights on a Titan position that would be at least parallel in stature. How she got it is another matter.

Lucas had a hard time figuring out how Sami could have ever qualified for a well-paying position with prestige and some amount of power too. It was not long after that this lonely lady with lots to offer the right man caught Franco's attention. He guided Sami into a makeover and lots more!

As long as Kate didn't want everyone in Salem to know about her call-girl past, Sami—who holds the blackmail photos—had certain job security and enormous leverage with Kate, until Sami was arrested for fatally shooting Franco.

their roller-coaster romance. After Jack and Eve married, the controlling interest went to Eve. Eventually, after that divorce, Jennifer used her trust fund money to buy back the stocks for Jack.

However, in 1992, when Jack wrongly believed that he was dying, he wanted to establish a financially secure base for Jennifer and sold the publication to Julie. Later, realizing he was in fine health, he wanted to buy it back. Eventually, he did.

However, he did so with money he found that had actually been a stash Billie hid for a criminal friend. That led to some tense times when the shady character wanted his money back from Billie.

Victor bought the newspaper in 1993, fired Jack, and added it to his Titan conglomerate.

Salem Tribune

Another traditional-format newspaper that is newer and has less circulation than either the *Chronicle* or *Spectator*. Although not a tabloid, it is more sensational than the *Chronicle* or *Spectator*. It is not nearly, however, as biting as *The Intruder*.

The Intruder

A typical tabloid in format and editorial style, it specializes in scandal.

During Billie Reed's trial for murder, its ace reporter, Fisher Andrews, covered the proceedings. Earlier, he also covered the Victor Kiriakis marriage to Kate Roberts with a headline that called the union "Kiriakis' Folly."

It was this newspaper that made Sami Brady look like a liar during Alan Harris' rape trial. Later, the newspaper also sensationalized Sami's self-defense shooting of her harasser with the 1995 headline: "Sami Brady Bobbittizes Alan Harris."

In her huge office with a view, Sami has the trappings of a smart business-woman. She knows power strategy and is learning about business. Having an office that's nice and bigger than Carrie's workspace was important to Sami.

In 1997, when Sami found photos of Kate working as a call girl, she took them to Bennett Price, another reporter at this tabloid.

Dr. Craig Wesley also instigated this newspaper to run a story about Laura's alleged mental/emotional instability when Mike was his adversary in running for the hospital's position of Chief of Staff.

The things that went on behind Sami's closed door ran the gamut. Even closets were not off limits for her sexual encounters with her lover, Franco.

Law Enforcement

Salem Police Department

Located on Front Street, the police, court, and prison complex has been the scene of trials and traumas for many residents and those just passing through. Yet it's also the rock-solid foundation for what's right in Salem. It is a place where, over the years, Abe Carver, Roman Brady, Shane Donovan, even Bo and Hope have fought crime and brought law and order to town.

The Ninth Precinct has its offices, booking rooms, holding cells, and coffee kitchenettes. The Detective division is located in Room 125.

For many years, Commissioner Samuels has been in charge.

In 1983, Bo Brady came zooming into town on his motorcycle. One of his first stops was his brother Roman's office. He delivered a wedding present—a microwave oven—to the new groom; and Roman's new bride, Marlena, often dropped in.

Shortly after the Brady Fish Market was robbed and Shawn was shot, Bo too became a police officer. Hope also passed the strenuous training and joined the force. All three Bradys—Roman, Bo, and Hope—have been in and out of their Salem Police Department positions periodically through the years. They have managed to mix international crime fighting with the ISA, personal time off (usually because of travel or kidnapping) and even a modeling career with their law enforcement endeavors. Careers here have been bumpy. Each has been suspended, or sometimes only suspended as cover for a clandestine operation.

In mid-1996, much of Sami's early panic over Will's kidnap was expressed at the station. She filed a report about her neighbor, Mary, stealing the child. Later, Marlena identified the woman as the same one she saw at the airport with a child Will's age. And there was Jill, in cahoots with Franco in some quirky way, who showed up apparently badly beaten. She alerted them to a problem on Smith Island, where soon after, Andre turned up dead with Franco standing over him. The crime remains an open case in police department files. Later, when Bo brought Franco to stand in a lineup for Jill, she failed to pick him out as her attacker, and he was cleared. She left town shortly thereafter.

The Police Department parking structure was the scene of a tragic accident. Hoping to keep Austin and Carrie from taking off on a short motor getaway, Sami borrowed Austin's car from outside the Brady Pub. He reported it stolen. Eventually, the police brought the car and Sami to the station. When Austin realized who had it and why, he decided not to press charges. However, in spite of Sami's insistence that there was something terribly wrong with the car, Austin slipped into the driver's seat and began to pull away. Unfortunately, the transmission dropped into reverse and slammed Sami repeatedly into the wall. Austin paid for that accident with many months of guilt and manipulation as Sami used her injuries and convalescence to further her own plans to snag Austin.

Inside the police station, Bo maneuvered, by means of high-

After many years, the police department updated their office facilities and Abe, after his promotion to Commander, got a refurbished office

tech laser devices, to steal some evidence out of Abe's office safe. Of course, it turned out that Bo was working undercover, and stealing from the P.D. was part of the plan to have him prove himself to drug lord J. L. King.

Later, a young drug-runner named Viper was brought to the interrogation room in connection with Shawn-Douglas' shooting. When Viper was killed rather than arrested, Bo was a suspect for a while. He was eventually cleared. The J. L. King drug case caused Bo all sorts of problems, especially his further estrangement from Hope when Billie got involved in the case and, through the pressure of King's manipulation, married Bo.

At the end of 1997 and into the next year, the station was the setting for further lies and their unraveling. Abe eventually explained to Hope that Bo had been working undercover during his seemingly romantic involvement with Billie. Stefano finally admitted Peter was alive. Max was arrested in connection with the King case.

Susan Blake was brought in for questioning when an opened letter carrying her fingerprints was discovered at the Blake house after Kristen was found dead in the pool. It was at the police station that Edmund proposed to Susan, not realizing it was actually Kristen in disguise. Laura too was brought in and accused of Kristen's murder, and was put through a hearing when she admitted going to the Blake house and firing shots at Kristen.

The Salem Jail

After Roman, Justin, and Adrienne banned together to successfully break Diane Colville out of her cell in the eighties, the prison underwent some security changes. In the course of the King escapade, Billie was arrested and, as a warning from King to Bo, stabbed by another inmate. King threatened that Hope could be next if he ever doubted Bo's loyalty.

Kristen, Vivian, and Ivan also found themselves in prison here after their hijinks in the DiMera mansion secret room regarding Marlena's kidnap. Kristen was released almost immediately. It took Vivian's last remaining money to pay fines for herself and Ivan. Stefano enjoyed some good music and chess during his incarceration. He allowed

Vivian and Ivan ended up in Salem's jail after Kate threw them out of the Kiriakis mansion and Stefano involved them in helping him hide from police.

himself to be caught and used the situation to bargain for his ultimate freedom. In exchange for delivering a cure for terminally ill Roman, Stefano would be a free man, with all past crimes erased. The tactic did not work with Abe, but John and Lexie managed to get the secret code and released him. After the jungle trek and the successful potion did its work, Roman was back to health and Stefano embarked on a new life, as a free citizen of Salem.

When Peter was held in jail after turning up alive and armed at a bogus memorial for Jennifer, Stefano visited him and gave him the cure for the jungle madness that was tormenting him. After Peter was sentenced, Stefano found him accommodations in a nicer prison in another city.

The Salem Courthouse

This is a great arena for the unveiling of secrets! With an inquisitive audience as well as jury, Billie was on trial in Courtroom Six for her father's murder. Much was learned about the Curtis family then. Billie's incestuous relationship became public; so did the fact that Kate had been legally married to Curtis until the time of his death. That meant Kate was reunited with her children, Billie and Austin; her marriage to Victor Kiriakis was invalid. During Alan Harris's trial on rape charges, Sami was humiliated and the animosity between her and Carrie was aggravated.

Later, in the summer of 1996, Austin and Carrie tried to sue Sami for custody of Will, but Sami managed to sway the judge in her favor. Furthermore, Sami later successfully got a restraining order against Carrie, keeping her one hundred feet away from her and Will. Jack was found guilty of killing Peter after Stefano blackmailed the judge into handing down a life's sentence in early 1997. He was retried after Stefano was known to be alive, thus giving some credibility to Laura's claim that Peter was alive too. However, Kristen lied under oath and claimed Peter was dead. Jack was sent back to prison.

Kristen drugged Susan into signing custody of Elvis over to her. However, in judge's chambers as the final paperwork was to be completed, John and Marlena helped Susan pull off a counterswitch, and posing as Kristen, Susan reclaimed Elvis and left the country.

Salem State Penitentiary

This facility has held a number of Salem residents. Liz Chandler was incarcerated here after nearly killing Marie Horton; Kayla Brady was imprisoned for the murder of Marina Toscano.

In more recent times, Jack's imprisonment offered the most intrigue. His cell-mate Travis turned out to be a DiMera spy and, when released, became Jennifer's neighbor Trent. Also, for a time, Jennifer used phony identification and a wig while posing as a guard at the prison and tried to help Jack uncover a history of abuse and underhanded dealings there. That led to some steamy scenes and threats against her from aggressive guards. When their plot was blown, Jack was nearly killed by a press machine and Trent kidnapped Jennifer, planning to deliver her to Peter. Jack made his successful prison break through a tunnel dug by another inmate.

After Sami borrowed Austin's car, he reported it stolen. She tried to tell him that there was a serious malfunction in the vehicle but he wouldn't listen. As he tried to leave the police department's parking structure, he ran down Sami.

The ever-elusive Stefano allowed himself to be imprisoned so he could negotiate a deal to save Roman Brady's life and ultimately earn his freedom from all past transgressions. The super-secure jail cell was equipped with stereo equipment and a chessboard.

Abe Carver, a high-ranking Salem law officer, found himself the son-in-law of Stefano DiMera and Celeste, Stefano's mistress, who tried her best to evade Stefano's wrath and yet help Abe and protect Lexie as best as possible. Police often called on her to track down Stefano in his many worldwide hiding places.

Salem University Medical Center

More than a health care center, the hospital has been close to the heart of Salem from the start. One of the town's most beloved patriarchs, the late Tom Horton, was Chief of Staff for many years before his demise. Presently, Tom's grandson, Dr. Mike Horton, has earned the position of Chief of Staff after a campaign against ambitious and dirty-dealing Dr. Craig Wesley. Although much like his grandfather in the respect he receives from his coworkers, Mike is a very eligible bachelor. That makes him a target for amorous nurses and a shoulder for Carrie, who is growing apart from husband Austin. It's that latter circumstance that might allow Dr. Wesley, and his scheming wife Nancy, to eventually have Mike removed from his position.

ER and ICUs

Certainly one of the most exciting places in Salem, almost every resident has passed through the Emergency Room at one time or another, as a patient or with a loved one in trouble. Too many have spent their time in an Intensive Care Unit as well.

After being badly beaten by a mystery attacker, whom Bo believed to be Franco, Jill was brought to the ER but managed to slip out. In her weak state, she was hit by a cab and returned to the ER unconscious. Hope happened to be a patient in the ER after an accident at the pier.

At the end of 1996, Sami was rushed to the ER after being repeatedly slammed by Austin's car. She survived surgery, but had a near-death experience. She went into the light but her connection to Will brought her back. She remained in a coma until repeated attempts by Austin using Will and the tape of their wedding finally brought her around. She was, however, paralyzed from the waist down and had no memory of the last four years. She remained in the hospital for several weeks before continuing her recuperation at home; she was still too fragile for people to tell her the truth of her deeds and a marriage that had nothing to do with Austin's true feelings about her.

In spring of 1997, after Shawn-Douglas was shot, he was brought in and treated. Bo and Hope kept vigil. When Billie and J. L. King showed up, drug lord King provided the ring and Bo and Billie became engaged—much to the confusion of Hope and Shawn-D.

In February 1997, Susan delivered Kristen and John's baby boy and married John in the delivery room, where Vivian helped Susan sign the marriage certificate with Kristen's name. Kristen, disguised as a nurse in surgical gown and mask, watched. Within a few days the newborn underwent heart surgery and survived.

Laura was brought in after an accidental overdose of drugs administered secretly by Lynn and Kristen. Lynn helped Laura escape when she learned Stefano planned to kidnap Marlena.

When Roman was unexpectedly returned to Salem, he was first brought to the ICU for tests and observation before Kristen was allowed to take him to the DiMera mansion to recuperate.

Turning points in early 1998 were Roman's bout of high blood pressure after seeing John and Marlena together, and Billie's post-fainting exam that was the first indication of her pregnancy. But Stefano's near-fatal heart attack was another piece of big news with major repercussions. It strengthened Lexie's loyalty, set Hope on a hunt for her past, and spurred Kristen to later confront Stefano and reveal herself as alive.

Belle was rushed here by Roman after she ingested penicillin in a candy intended for Marlena by scheming Kristen.

After a car accident, Laura was brought in for an examination. Then she was brought into the police rooms for questioning in Kristen's death.

When Caroline Brady was hospitalized with a heart problem, it was easily corrected. However, as one of Dr. Carly Manning's patients, crazed and vengeful Vivian nearly killed her with a syringe of cleaning fluid.

Dr. Bader was Sami Brady's maternity doctor before becoming Kristen's, Susan's, and Billie's obstetrician too.

It was Austin's devotion, based on guilt more than love, that pulled Sami through the worst moments. He and baby Will gave Sami reason to live.

Laura has spent many days and nights in the hospital as a practicing psychiatrist and as a patient. This time Stefano had erased her most recent memory with a laser procedure after Laura discovered him with a very-much-alive Peter. Nurse Lynn was also on Stefano's payroll and kept Laura medicated after Laura started remembering a little too much.

Spending more time with Carrie was a mixed blessing for Mike, who had already fallen in love with her before she married Austin.

Carrie's efforts helped Mike land the Chief of Staff position, but Dr. Craig and his crafty wife, Nancy, continued to manipulate problems that would threaten Mike's career and Carrie's marriage.

The Morgue

Technically a place for the dead, this area has been a lively site over the years.

After many weeks of exorcism rites, Marlena appeared to be dead and was brought to the morgue, which ultimately became the battleground for John's last stand against the devil. John won; Marlena lived.

When Andre's body lay here after he was killed on Smith Island, Franco paid him a visit and placed blue contact lenses in his eyes so he'd fit the description of Jill's attacker.

After Peter seemed to have died when his heart failed, his remains were moved into the morgue. There, Stefano waited to revive Peter and take him to a secret place to recuperate. Stefano's schedule was momentarily delayed when Celeste found her way into the morgue to say good-bye to Peter.

Following an autopsy on Kristen's body, the coroner told Abe, Roman, Marlena, John, and Stefano that Kristen had a lot of drugs and alcohol in her before drowning. Since there were no signs of foul play, the initial ruling was that Kristen died a suicide.

Medical Offices

Various doctors base their practice at SMC, including Mike, Marlena, and Laura, who each have their own office.

In Marlena's hospital office, Susan became a client, particularly concerned over an evil woman who stole her child and husband. In addition to words of advice, Marlena gave Susan a special stone to hold when she was feeling especially tense. That stone helped lead Marlena to the truth of the situation when she found it at the DiMera mansion.

By summer 1997, after Carrie and Austin went off to honeymoon in Rome, Sami talked Mike into hiring her as an assistant in his office. She used her position to manipulate him into going to a medical conference in Rome.

During Kristen's faked pregnancy, Susan was examined instead of Kristen on a number of occasions.

Records Room

Hospital records, whether on paper or in a computer, seem as easy to access here as a book from the library.

In late 1996, Sami was rushed to surgery after being accidentally rammed by Austin's car. During the surgery, Austin and Carrie found solace and prayed for Sami in the hospital chapel. Sami, however, got closer to God when she momentarily left this life and entered the light.

Vivian discovered that Kristen had two different blood types in her file.

Sami, who first saw Will's blood type mentioned on material sent to her at home, visited the records room and discovered that Lucas, not Austin, was the father of her son, Will. She had hoped to change the records in the hospital files, but was not able to. Later, Carrie and Eric managed to get into the files and found the truth of Will's paternity in time to stop the wedding between Sami and Austin.

The Chapel

This has been a place for many people to seek solace in their time of pain. Here, when Marlena came to pray, she overheard John's prayers. He appealed to heaven that Marlena wouldn't love him so that he could be a proper husband to Kristen and father to their baby.

While Roman was hospitalized and his demise seemed certain, he and Marlena were about to wed in the chapel; but John, Stefano, Kristen, and Hope arrived with the cure before vows were exchanged.

Part Four

Salem Hot Spots

Hotels, Restaurants, Bars, and Clubs

Salem Inn

An impressive, large building ten floors high, it is primarily brick, stone, and wood. The rooms are quaint; the restaurant and lounges are elegant without being stuffy; and there are meeting rooms for banquets, business seminars, and conventions.

Back in 1987 when Alex Marshall owned the main hotel in Salem, he set it on fire for the insurance money. It was later renovated and reopened.

In the fall of 1997, Carrie and Austin tried to enjoy a honeymoon suite here as best they could. Sami called Austin out to the Kiriakis mansion. Mike stopped by to keep Carrie company when he heard she was left alone. When she spilled

After their harrowing experiences with Jude
kidnapping Hope, the return home was a blessing.
Bo finally told Hope he still loves her and arranged
a celebration at the Salem Club where friends like
Abe were happy to see them together and others,
like Kristen and John, were working on rewriting
their own love story.

It was a rough time for Lucas Reed and Mike Horton
when they learned that they were half-brothers
because Kate had an affair with Bill Horton many
years ago. Still, as they ran into each other at places
like The Cheatin' Heart, they began to soften their
edgy attitudes toward each other.

John and Marlena's engagement party at the Penthouse Grille was filled with well-wishers and plenty of drama.

Vivian was forced by Stefano to bring an inappropriate Phoenix gift.

Sami and Lucas continued to scheme to keep Carrie and Austin apart, even while Sami hides her returned memory and the fact that Lucas is Will's dad.

At the Penthouse Grille New Year's party, Franco and Kate connived against Sami. With his first dance with Sami, he had her charmed.

Austin was enjoying a night out for dinner at Chez Vous when he was called away to talk to Billie. He asked Mike to come over and keep Carrie company, unaware of the growing attraction between the two.

A few months later, guilt-ridden Mike forced himself to start dating. He brought nurse Ali to Chez Vous, but there was only a fleeting romance.

Oh-so-charming Franco led Sami blindly into a swanky suite, and down the path of false hopes and dreams. He wanted citizenship and she wanted happily-ever-after. Eventually, he ended up dead, and Sami went to trial for killing him. But she didn't kill Franco, Lucas did.

champagne on her nightgown, she showered while Mike dried the gown. Austin returned to find Carrie in a towel, and Mike holding her gown.

John, who had sold or leased out his loft, moved into the hotel after Roman was cured and while the two men were still rivals over Marlena, who remained in her penthouse. After Kristen's apparent death in early 1998, John found a good-bye message on his answering machine that could be interpreted as a suicide message.

The Continental Hotel

A classy older establishment, the hotel has been around for decades. Its restaurant is popular among the old money in town. It also has a charming bar often used as a meeting place for Salem residents who want some privacy away from usual hangouts.

The Cheatin' Heart

A country-style beer bar and dance hall with a few pool tables, this nightspot is a comfy and casual place to kick back and have some relaxed fun along with the well known chili.

In the past, Emmy and Adrienne were both waitresses here; Chuck and Jimbo still periodically tend bar. Steve used to do pretty well as a pool player, making enough money to support himself at times. Even Tom and Alice joined Calliope here for a few racks in the late eighties.

In October of 1993, after discovering that he was possibly at least partially responsible for daughter Abby's aplastic anemia because he signed some toxic waste variance years ago, Jack got drunk with Billie at this bar. He went home, said good-bye to a sleeping Jennifer, and pinned a St. Christopher's medal on Abby's blanket before abruptly leaving Salem.

Billie won a fledgling fragrance company, Countess Wilhelmina, in a pool game several years ago.

This is where Sami slipped Austin the drug that kept him pliable but not passed out as she got him back to his apartment and maneuvered him into making love to her.

Very European Franco Kelly first caught the ladies' eyes when he was discovered at this very American-style bar in the summer of 1996. Hope and Wendy, while dates Bo and Jonah were off for a moment, had just commented that they were happy with their men when Franco walked by and caught their attention. After Bo left, a stranger rudely approached Hope and Franco intervened, then

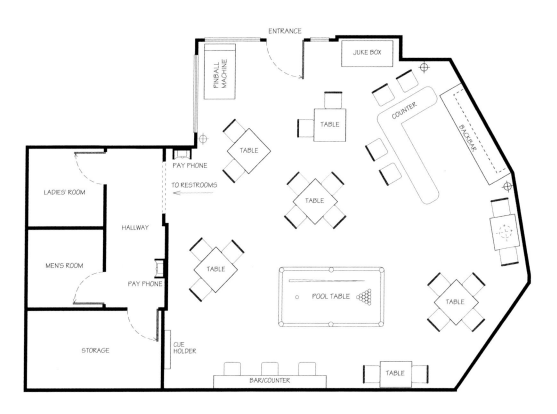

CHEATIN' HEART

stayed with her until Bo returned. She taught him how to do the two-step. Bo was suspicious of Franco from the first moment. Franco and Hope later met again at a photo shoot.

Penthouse Grille

Atop the Titan Publishing building, this elegant restaurant is owned by Victor Kiriakis.

Victor and Kate Roberts wed here in September of 1993. Later, they learned the marriage was invalid because her ex-husband, Curtis, was still alive.

In 1994, Bill Horton unexpectedly showed up at his mother's Celebration of Faith party. Except for his ex-wife, Laura, everyone was happy to see him.

The same year, enemies Kate and Vivian were trapped for hours in a stalled elevator car during a blackout.

A year after Kate disappeared in a plane over the sea and was presumed dead, Vivian threw a memorial gala. It was also a benefit to raise funds for a hospital pediatric wing in Kate's honor.

Within a very short time, Kate—very much alive—returned to Salem. After exposing both Vivian and Sami, she planned to help her children find happiness with the people they loved. She gladly hosted Austin and Carrie's engagement party at the Penthouse Grille and surprised them with a trip to Paris.

Another engagement party a year later was even more exciting. John and Marlena were celebrating their betrothal after Kristen and Susan were exposed. Vivian, as arranged by Stefano, arrived with a large Phoenix statue as a very inappropriate gift for the couple. Stefano, disguised as a waiter, savored the moment as he planned to kidnap Marlena. Kristen, still delusional and obsessed with John, thought the party was a birthday celebration for her. She crashed it, and when reality hit, she threatened to jump off the terrace. John talked her down. Stefano was furious that Kristen ruined his plans.

Several months later, after Kristen

1997–1998 New Year's Eve party at the Penthouse Grille

"I Say a Little Prayer"

"I Care About You"

"Building a Mystery"

"CoCo Jamboo"

"Falling"

"Nobody Knows"

"Love is Alive"

"Never, Never Gonna Give You Up"

"Two Become One"

brought ailing Roman back to Salem, forcing Marlena and John to play out roles to make Roman comfortable, the foursome—John and Kristen, Marlena and Roman—dined tensely together. When John finally walked out, Kristen said she and her "husband" were going through a difficult time.

Many Salem residents started 1998 at the New Year Gala. Several passed out, but not from drinking. Billie fainted and soon discovered she was pregnant with Bo's child. Roman collapsed before he could confront Marlena and John about the newly learned truth of their relationship; it was high blood pressure.

In the alley after the party, Sami was mugged, but heroic Franco saved her and paid off the "mugger." It was the start of a new cycle in their relationship, one that would have Sami off balance for a change.

By spring, after treating Sami to a makeover, Franco helped her show off her new look with a romantic evening at the Penthouse Grille. Roman, Marlena, Edmund, and Susan were dining together there. Lucas, drinking heavily, was with mom Kate. Carrie and Austin were there too. On the dance floor Franco kissed Sami and Lucas felt a pang of jealousy. Soon after, he confronted Sami and called her a slut and Franco belted him. Roman too was watching over Sami and warned Franco not to toy with Sami's feelings. It was at the Grille that Edmund sprang a surprise wedding on Susan, who was actually presumed-dead Kristen in disguise.

Chez Vous

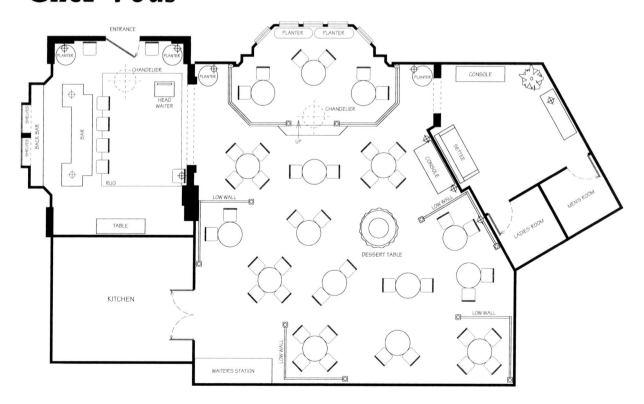

This fine and fancy French restaurant is perfect for couples who want a healthy serving of romance and privacy with their dining.

When Sami knew Carrie and Mike were having dinner here, she sent Austin to get take-out so he would see them together.

Blue Note

A classy little piano bar, it was first seen when Roman came here to listen to some quiet jazz and nurse his blues after setting Marlena free to follow her heart with John. Billie popped in too, and the duo commiserated over their lost loves and reminisced about their own shared experience in Paris.

Salem Club

Although around quite some time, this club regained popularity in 1996. Jonah, Wendy, Abe, and Lexie celebrated the anniversary of the night Abe proposed to Lexie. This almost prompted Jonah to propose to Wendy, but he got cold feet.

John joined the group and when Marlena came by, he asked her to dance "for old time sake," but it was clear their chemistry was still very powerful.

In early 1997, Vivian—suspecting something afoul, but totally unaware of what—followed Susan (disguised as Kristen) and saw her go into the ladies' room. Very shortly after, the real Kristen joined Vivian, who had sat down at the bar. Confused by Kristen's sudden arrival, Vivian never noticed Susan, in her own clothes and hairdo, leave the ladies' room.

It was here Bo sat drowning his sorrows over losing Hope and appeared drunk when he got into a minor brawl with Abe. Later, it was revealed to be staged to provide Abe a reason to have Bo dismissed from the Salem Police Department. It was a ploy to set up the "disgruntled ex-cop" as a prime target for drug dealer J. L. King. It worked. Unsuspecting J. L. pressured Bo into working for him, not discovering until much later that Bo was working undercover.

In early 1998, Sami and Franco were trying to get Austin's attention by making him jealous. The scheming couple showed up and danced, then kissed. It was

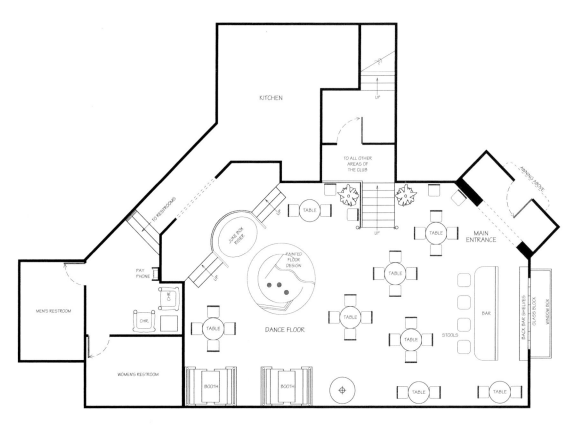

SALEM CLUB

the first time Sami realized she was feeling—as much as she wanted to dismiss it—some serious attraction for Franco.

Sami's attraction to Franco and his seductive ways blinded her to his manipulations. He was only interested in her as a means to stay in the United States. With a contract on his life issued by a crime family in Italy, and a counterfeit green card, which meant deportation, Franco had to marry a U.S. citizen in a hurry. To save his life, Franco proposed to Sami and she accepted. He continued to lead the life of a single man away from his fiancée and was nearly trapped by Sami, who secretly set him up with a beautiful model, but he caught on at the last minute and dismissed the woman. However, Austin discovered his dates with stripper, Candy Lace, and told Sami of Franco's infidelity on their wedding day. Franco met his end when he nearly clobbered Kate with an andiron because she was going to turn him in to the INS and Lucas shot him. Sami was charged with the murder.

Brady Pub

Established in the summer of 1992 by Shawn and Caroline Brady, it had previously been the Brady Fish Market until robbers trashed the place and shot Shawn, only wounding him. The store was remodeled and the new business was financed by John. He had strong attachments to the people and the place. When he stumbled into town as the Pawn, it was the first place he ventured into. The Brady family became his own when he was mistaken for Roman for many years.

About six months earlier, Steve "Patch" Johnson was seen in the fish market on his first day in Salem in June of 1985.

Now the market is the Brady Pub, a casual and often fun place where family and friends celebrate birthdays, engagements, St. Patrick's Day, and other happy times with gusto and impromptu song. They have also gathered here for solace after more than one funeral and for strength during Satan's plagues.

The most noted item on the menu is the famous Brady Clam Chowder, made from a recipe handed down from Shawn's grandfather. Along with Shawn and Caroline, longtime waitress Lisa is a happy, familiar face. At times, Wendy and Jamie also worked as waitresses here.

The Park Café

This is a cute café across from University Hospital that was popular in the late 1980s.

The Sand Dollar

Popular in the early nineties, it's on the Salem riverfront near the shopping district. Jack and Jennifer's engagement party was held here.

Bruce & Jack's

When "pregnant" Kristen needed to get rid of John for a few hours, she had him run around to several places to fill her sudden food urges. Well across town, this shop is where she sent him for some ice cream—chocolate chip cookie dough.

Lu's Chinese Restaurant

Kristen insisted on Moo Goo Gai Pan specifically from this restaurant.

Irv's Deli

This was John's third stop that same night. Kristen claimed to love their pickles.

Snake Pit

A dark and sleazy chic place, it's J. L. King's enterprise and front for his drug operation.

Hope, Billie, and Jennifer were among a well-meaning group of Salem residents who attended a charity event at the club. It was, however, just another way of intimidating Bo, letting him know how close J. L. could get to Bo's family and friends.

At J. L.'s insistence, Bo spent far too much time in the drug boss' office. Billie made the mistake of snooping, and after being found hiding in a closet here, she became part of Bo's undercover assignment.

It was in J. L.'s office that Bo, held at gunpoint, learned there was a bomb planted at the Horton house. Some fast talking allowed him to be set free and defuse the bomb in time.

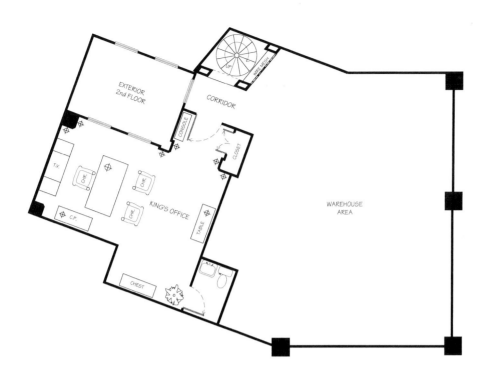

KING'S OFFICE @ THE SNAKE PIT

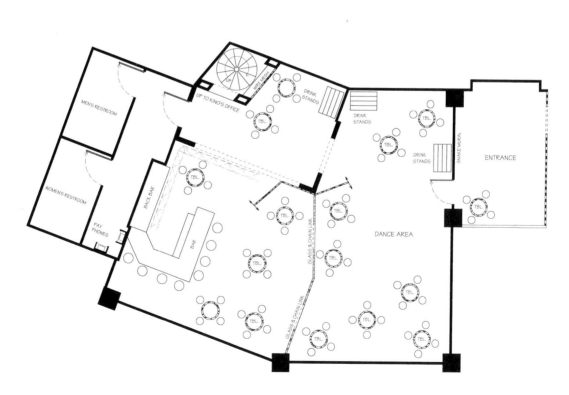

THE SNAKE PIT

Casey's Roadhouse

A beer joint that sometimes attracts some rough patrons.

During a bout with her multiple personality disorder, Kimberly (as red-haired Lacey) frequented this bar. Here she met an aggressive guy, Randy, who got her into the nearby woods, accused her of teasing her, and would have raped her had she not killed him in self-defense.

When Billie Reed first arrived in Salem in 1993, it was also one of her favorite hangouts.

The Blue Moon was the center of drug trade and romantic intrigue and where Franco made headway keeping Bo and Hope apart for Billie.

Blue Moon

This club, owned by Peter, was reconstructed from an old warehouse. Plenty of shady dealings transpired here and Jude St. John was one of Peter's hired hands.

In an attempt to find out more of what went on here, Hope went undercover as a stripper. This investigation was her last police assignment.

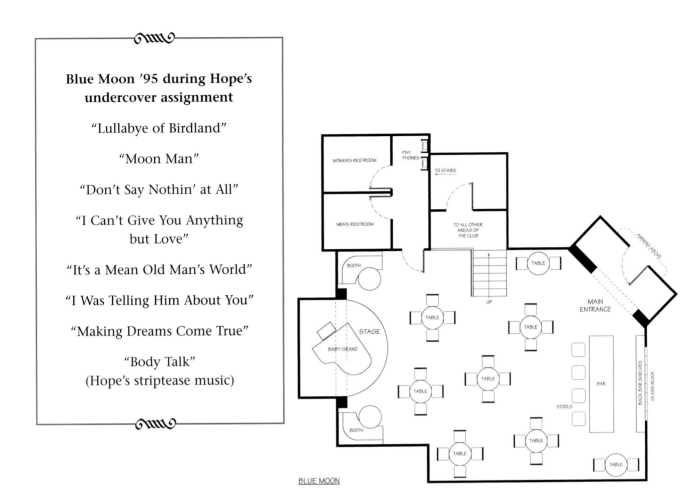

Blue Moon '95 during Hope's
undercover assignment

"Lullabye of Birdland"

"Moon Man"

"Don't Say Nothin' at All"

"I Can't Give You Anything
but Love"

"It's a Mean Old Man's World"

"I Was Telling Him About You"

"Making Dreams Come True"

"Body Talk"
(Hope's striptease music)

BLUE MOON

Blue Cat

In this seedy nightclub, Steve Olson ran drug deals in the late seventies.

Shenanigans

Owned by Trish Clayton and run by Chris Kositchek, this comfortable and casual restaurant held a gala masquerade party for its 1982 opening. Chris' house specialty item was Peanut Butter Burgers. Danny Grant worked for Chris and Trish.

In the early nineties the place was bought by Alice Horton and run with the help of her daughter-in-law Maggie. They renamed it Alice's Restaurant, and proceeds benefited the Salem University Hospital. Ginger Dawson worked as the head waitress here.

The building also has two apartments, one above and one below the restaurant. Steve, Nick, Bo and Hope, Justin and Adrienne, Frankie and Max, and Carly all lived in the building at different times.

Twilight Bar

This popular place was bought by Tony DiMera in 1981. It had been previously owned by Stuart Whyland. Trish Clayton was the manager and Danny Grant was a bartender.

Beefcakes

A popular male "exotic dance" club popular in the early eighties. It's where Pete Jannings got a job shedding his clothes to music. He hoped to put together enough money so he and Melissa Anderson could leave town together. However, he got Ivy Selejko pregnant and married her.

Jump!

Pete owned and operated this dance club. Many years later, it became the Salem Club.

Beat Bar

Owned and operated by Calliope, it opened in 1989 and lasted barely more than a year. Ethan Reilly, Calliope's boyfriend, helped her out. One of the best attractions was Norm dePlume, really Dr. Tom Horton, who did poetry readings.

Sergio's / Doug's Place

Addie bought this restaurant in 1974 and renamed it Doug's Place for her new husband, Doug Williams, who often sang for guests having dinner. Addie was the hostess. After Addie's death, Doug remodeled the place and his friend Robert started singing with him. A very young Hope spent a lot of time here until she went to boarding school for a short time. It was eventually closed when Doug's license was revoked after Larry Atwood conned him into an illegal gambling operation.

Wings

This was perhaps Salem's longest-established restaurant and club, surviving several owners and remodelings. Originally called Doug's Place on the Lake, it was opened in his wife, Julie's, name. Before Doug and Julie left for Europe in 1986, It was sold to Dr. Neil Curtis, who renamed it Blondies as a gift for Liz Chandler, who sang there on a regular basis. Dave was the maître d' and Calliope was the hostess.

Eventually, it was bought by Nick and renamed Wings in tribute to Eve and her favorite song, "The Wind Beneath My Wings." April managed the club for Nick until he was murdered in 1990. He left the club to Julie. That same year, the restaurant managed to survive a terrible storm in spite of part of the roof falling in and the main level flooding.

Julie continued to run the club until she left town to rejoin Doug in early 1993. Tanner Scofield worked here as a bartender and Molly Brinker was the hostess, while Dave continued as maître d'. Emilio and Melissa often sang at the club during Julie's ownership. After Julie left Salem, the club was managed for a time by Maggie.

Shortly after Austin Reed's arrival in Salem in late 1992, he played piano at Wings and caught the eye of Carrie Brady. At first she thought the woman singing "Come Rain or Come Shine" was Austin's girlfriend, but it turned out to be his sister, Billie.

The last time Wings was noticed, Doug and Julie, back in Salem after Gina/Hope returned, visited the club. Here in early 1994, although it was closed, Doug provided a very romantic evening, singing "The Most Beautiful Girl in the World," their signature love song.

Part Five

Beyond Salem

Red Dragon Inn

Aremid

Stefano DiMera raised Peter and Rachel Blake here after he orchestrated the untimely death of their father and, accidentally, seemed to have also killed their mother. She eventually turned out to be the mysterious, troubled Woman in White, whose hidden presence haunted the town for decades. She was not pleased with Peter and Jennifer intruding upon Blake house in late 1995. Later, she became reunited with Kristen and Peter and became an ally to many people who were not in Stefano's camp.

Many Salemites first came to this town and its environs because of Jennifer and Peter's wedding. Tony DiMera's diabolical suicide, framing John for murder, brought others too. A town bearing the DiMera name spelled backward was bound to hold trouble. There was plenty more: John was nearly put to death in the gas chamber; Lexie discovered her true parentage; and Hope was lost in an avalanche and abducted in nearby mountains.

No matter how many character witnesses were called, no matter the testimony of people present, the judge was in DiMera's service.

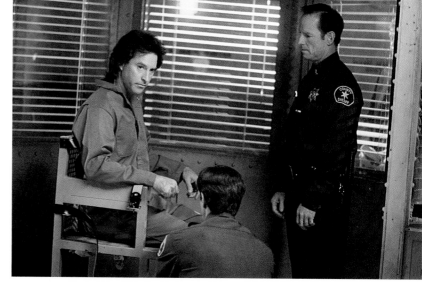

The gas pellets had already been dropped before Tony's journal was rushed to the chamber with the proof to set John free.

After several attempts at finding Hope even after no one thought she could be alive, Bo saved her from Jude, who was keeping her captive. He recuperated at the Red Dragon Inn until he was strong enough to go home.

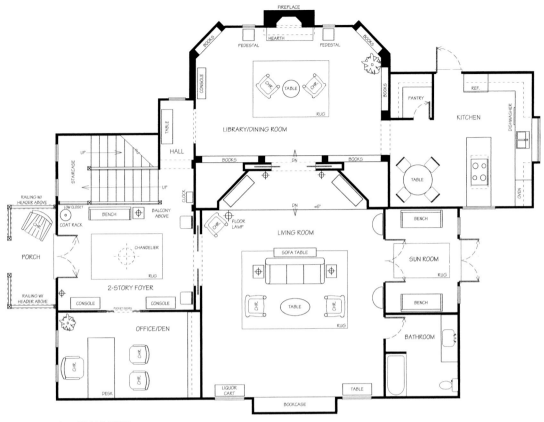

AREMID MANSION
MAIN LEVEL

AREMID MANSION
SECOND LEVEL

The Blake House

Tony DiMera, already suffering a fatal illness and insanely jealous over Kristen and John, put together an intricate suicide plot that framed John for murder. In the library, Tony rigged John's gun on a bookshelf, placed gunpowder on a door handle, and set up an argument between himself and John before actually shooting himself. Had he not recorded his plans in his diary, John would have been put to death for murder.

Here John, Abe, and Bo planned a romantic evening for their special women: Kristen, Lexie, and Hope. The couples dressed in eighteenth-century attire and danced the evening away.

In his private room here, Stefano was counseled by Marlena, who was trying to help him regain his memory, which he lost when he was pitched from Marlena's penthouse. One night a rain came up while he was outside and he was hit by lightning. Stefano was brought back into the Blake house by Celeste. He regained his memory but kept it hidden for a while.

In the attic Lexie and Abe found an old newspaper dated the day Lexie was born. There was also news of a car accident; the woman who raised Lexie was involved in a hit-and-run accident that took place in front of the Aremid orphanage.

Stefano entertained Celeste with a candlelight dinner in the library, decorated with flowers.

Stefano plotted to have John sentenced to death. The Woman in White took Tony's diary from Stefano's room, but Stefano later found her secret hiding place and recovered it. He was stunned to find out Tony framed John for his murder.

Marlena and the Woman in White worked together to retrieve the diary. Marlena distracted Stefano with her seductive charms and snatched the diary, which she passed to her cohort through a window.

After Tony's death, Stefano knocked Marlena out with a sedative in the dining room and began his kidnap plot.

Red Dragon Inn

Run by Lou and his niece Sara, the multipurpose facility, a bar-restaurant-hotel, offered rooms for wedding guests and a basement jail cell for John when he was arrested for Tony's murder.

On Valentine's Day Kristen brought imprisoned John a gift, an antique Victrola she had ordered earlier that was intended for their newlywed house.

Another time, Kristen visited John wearing only a sexy teddy outfit under her coat.

In one of the boarding rooms above the bar and restaurant, Jennifer became aware of her mother's fleeting, long-past affair with Jack.

Bo appealed to Hope to forgive him for not believing she was herself, not Gina, when she first returned to Salem from Maison Blanche.

Mike Horton locked Bo in a room here to keep him from renewing his search for Hope, who was lost in the mountains after an avalanche. Bo also was tended here after being shot by Jude. By then, Hope was at his side.

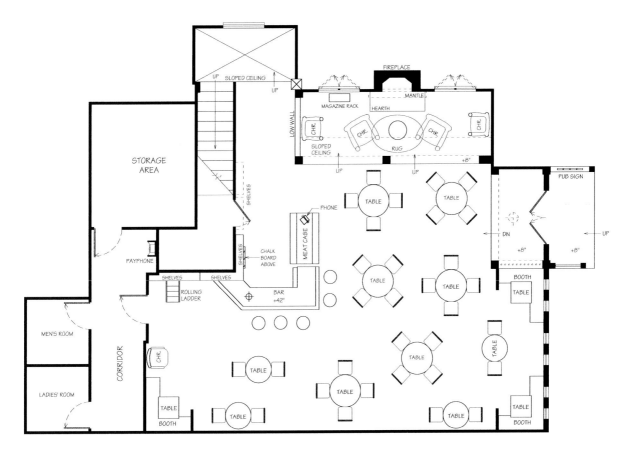

RED DRAGON

Courthouse, Prison, and Death Row

John was tried for the murder of Tony DiMera and sentenced to death by a judge blackmailed by Stefano. In the middle of the trial, Hope was lost on the ski slopes after an avalanche. Proceedings were briefly postponed so John could join the search for her.

In his days after conviction, John was held at a larger facility, on death row. While waiting to die, John wrote Marlena a love letter that she did not actually receive until many months later.

On his execution day, he was strapped to a chair in the gas chamber. Jack arrived not a moment too soon with Tony's tell-all diary, which he got from the Woman in White, and John was saved.

Dear Marlena,

If you are reading this letter, then I have been executed. No man is without sin, but God knows that I did not kill Tony. I have gone with the faith that death is not the end but a summons to a new existence, a summons to live with God in Paradise.

Of course, I feel that my time has come too soon. But God works in mysterious ways. I leave with few regrets. One is that my children will never know their father. The other one is leaving you, Doc.

I know that our life together has been complicated. You've been in love with other men, and I've been in love with other women. But the love we shared was something special, Doc. There never was and never could be anyone to fill that special place you hold in my heart.

I love you. I know now I always have, and I always will.

John

Newspaper, Orphanage, and Cemetery

With some research at Aremid newspaper archives and some help from the Parrot Man, Lexie gathered clues to her past. The Parrot Man showed her the graves of her supposed birth parents and she discovered they had died over a century ago. The names she had were clearly bogus. At the orphanage, she was not allowed access to adoption records, but Parrot Man (really Logan Michaels, who used to work at the orphanage) got her file for her and she found that Celeste was her mother; her father's name was not listed. Lexie had been adopted by Grace Brooks, Lexie's sister. Later, at the cemetery again, Lexie came upon Celeste, and Parrot Man came along. He made Celeste show Lexie the photo she, Celeste, held in her hand. It was, indeed, Stefano.

Mountain Area

When he was sought in connection with illegal activities at the Blue Moon and a link to Peter's criminal connections, Jude St. Clair hid in the mountains outside of Aremid. Bo and Hope decided to go skiing, unaware that Jude was in the area, plotting revenge against Hope for blinding one eye. After an avalanche buried Hope, Jude dug her out and held her in a remote cabin for weeks.

Bo and Shawn-Douglas placed a wreath on the mountain. When a bird landed on it, Bo took it as a sign Hope was still alive, but soon after mourned her as dead. Then he took up the search again, this time getting lost too.

Jack tried to capture Jude. They were fighting when Peter shot Jude, keeping him from revealing Peter's crime connections.

Caves and Tunnels

These are accessible through a hidden door in the master bedroom and lead to several places around Aremid. Stefano took Marlena through secret passages to a beach area to wait for his helicopter. Celeste followed them. When Stefano refused to take her along too, his long-time companion told him that he has a daughter, Lexie. Within minutes, Lexie arrived and tried to convince him to stay. A cave-in changed the situation and he got away with Marlena until John caught up with his small boat. Marlena was saved; Stefano escaped.

Aremid

BO AND HOPE

"Sophisticated Lady"

"Goodnight My Love" (dance and kiss at midnight, New Years '96)

STEFANO AND MARLENA'S DINNER DATE

Debussy's "Serenade" (Marlena turns down dancing)

Borodin's "Serenade for String Orchestra" (during dinner while the Woman in White starts a fire and Marlena hopes to find Tony's diary to save John from execution)

JOHN AND KRISTEN

"Embraceable You" (Kristen brought an old record player and champagne to entertain John in his cell)

JOHN AND MARLENA

"Love Won't Let Me Wait" (John thinks of Marlena)

"In a Perfect World" (they think of each other)

The Paris Masquerade

In the summer of 1996, with Kristen's help, Stefano managed to abduct Marlena. He took her to his underground lair in Paris. There he kept his Queen of the Night in a gilded cage, hoping that in time he would win her over. He intended to marry her and the two would rule as monarchs over the loyal but odd assortment of followers he had in his dark kingdom.

Things didn't go as Stefano planned. A doctor told Stefano that Marlena was deeply depressed and on the verge of dying. Hoping to lift her spirits, Stefano allowed Marlena to use his high-tech goggles to see Belle in Salem. The gesture backfired when Marlena only became more upset seeing her daughter and then watching Kristen comfort John. Later, Stefano realized that someone else had found the other goggles and was using them.

With so much time on her hands, Marlena wrote many pages a day in her journal. Her thoughts frequently turned to John and how terribly Kristen had manipulated him and everyone around them. She wrote:

To know that you will spend the rest of your life with Kristen is more pain than I can bear. She has built her life with you on lies and deceptions. I hope, I pray, that you will see the evil in her before too long.

Kristen is so desperate to hold on to you she told Stefano which plane I would be on so he could kidnap me. You kept that information from everybody but Kristen and she told Stefano. That time he failed, but for all I know she helped him again and he succeeded.

Stefano is becoming more unstable every day. He has progressed from obsession to madness. He cannot understand or accept the fact that I will never return his love, that I will never willingly make love with him, that we will never live happily ever after together.

I don't think he'll ever physically hurt me, but as he sinks deeper and deeper into fantasy I can't predict what could happen. I must find a way to escape. But how? It has been impossible so far, but I can't give up hope. I can't bear the thought of never seeing my children, my family, my friends again.

Trying to dislodge John from Marlena's mind and heart, Stefano gave her a newspaper with a fake headline about John's death. In her despair, Marlena agreed not to try to escape when Stefano released her from her boudoir prison. To seal her promise, Stefano warned her that he would harm her family if she tried anything during their outing to the street fair above them. In costumes, Stefano and Marlena strolled the fair, but Vivian and Ivan, who were there on vacation, spotted them. This gave Vivian the idea that if she could get Stefano to sign an affidavit that she did not willingly help him get out of Salem, she could go home without fear of being imprisoned.

Vivian knew her old lover only as Rudolpho. She was thrilled to see him in Salem but was stunned to discover his real identity, Stefano DiMera. His undercover tactics served his plan to hide from the police until he could abduct Marlena and flee to Paris. Vivian's unwitting involvement later landed her in jail.

Meanwhile, Marlena agreed to bed Stefano in turn for her freedom, but coyly put off his advances, buying time. She didn't know it, but John was already on his way to Paris; when Stefano found out, he sent a fax to Kristen, pretending to be John, suggesting that she join him in Paris. It was an invitation she would never dream of refusing. Soon after she arrived, John spotted Stefano, but Kristen feigned abdominal pain and he stayed with her instead.

In a church, John found a tapestry that he recognized from the game Kristen used to play with Stefano. It contained a map to the fabled Paris underground hidden tunnels, and John's instincts told him Stefano was holding Marlena there. He also figured out that the goal of the game, stealing the crown for the Queen of the Night, could lure Stefano out of hiding. At a costume ball, Marie Antoinette's crown would be on display. Of course, when Stefano learned of the event, he arranged to take Marlena. In her cell, Marlena managed to write a letter to her daughter, Belle, and hoped to pass it to someone at the ball.

Dearest Belle,

When I held you in my arms on the day of your birth, I was filled with a joy I'd never known. Every moment we've shared increased my joy. I cannot express the pain I feel being separated from you. I am doing all I can to get home to you.

Stefano realized that the ball was really a trap set by John, but Stefano had his own plan in mind. For starters, he made certain that there would be several masked women of Marlena's size wearing the same gold gown as the Queen wore in the game. He also had another man pose as Rene, John's friend. Before the night was over, even though John had Abe's help too, Stefano had indeed stolen the crown.

Arriving at the ball in a lush golden gown, Marlena was appalled to see so many other women in identical regalia. It was no fashion faux pas; Stefano tricked John and his cohorts when he made certain Marlena would be hidden among the obvious.

When Marlena came face-to-face with Kristen, the two argued. Soon after, John found Marlena in a hall at the palace, but Stefano stabbed a needle into John and drugged him before dragging him into the underground kingdom. There John was put on trial and found guilty of conspiring to kidnap their Queen. John was sentenced to death by guillotine. As John was about to be beheaded, Marlena broke free and placed her head above John's. The move only delayed the execution. Again, the blade was about to fall when suddenly Vivian and Ivan literally "dropped in," and in the confusion, Vivian saved John, allowing him and Marlena to run for the tunnels.

Rachel and Kristen were searching through the tunnels when an explosion buried them. Abe and Lexie managed to free them and they resumed their search for John and Marlena. John turned the tables on Stefano and held a gun on him while Marlena was very weak and sick from her confinement. When John asked Rachel to take his gun and watch Stefano while he carried Marlena, Stefano ran off and Rachel chased him. Those two ended up in a dead-end tunnel that contained a tankful of some explosive. Stefano warned Rachel that shooting him there would cause the tank to explode and kill them both. Rachel ripped off the veil she wore over her scarred face and Stefano was horrified. Rachel said aloud that what she was about to do was for the children's sake as she fired the gun, fully intending to kill Stefano regardless of her own fate. She and Stefano were buried in the rubble and presumed dead.

After everyone was out of the tunnels, Kristen was hospitalized and told she had lost her baby. Kristen blamed Marlena and her own mother, Rachel, for the loss and vowed not to lose John too. She then blackmailed a doctor into keeping her secret. Unaware of the miscarriage, Marlena agreed to keep silent about Kristen helping Stefano kidnap her until after Kristen's baby was born. Marlena had the baby's welfare in mind. Meanwhile, a nun found Marlena's journal with a list of Kristen's wrongdoings outlined in it and eventually returned it to Marlena.

Rather belatedly, Jack came to Paris to help his friends. Peter also came when

Kristen's presence distracted John and ultimately changed the course of their relationship when she miscarried their child and kept it a secret.

Off with his head! Evil king of the underground, Stefano, nearly got his wish.

Abe and Lexie, in equally sumptuous gala attire, were among the Salem residents who joined John in his mission to rescue Marlena.

he heard about Kristen being in the hospital and the loss of their mother. Peter was unaware that Daniel Scott was also hiding out in Paris. When he threw Jennifer a birthday party at a French restaurant, Daniel almost attended as Celeste's date.

Austin and Carrie had gone to France for a prehoneymoon holiday through the countryside and planned to marry in Paris. Carrie bought a dress at Madame Yvette's Salon and the couple were about to wed when they got word that Will had been kidnapped by Sami's neighbor, Mary, in Salem. Their plans came to a halt. They didn't realize that the baby they heard crying at their hotel had indeed been Will. They had been that close!

At the same time, Billie, who had been living in Europe promoting Countess Wilhelmina cosmetics, met Carrie and Austin at a café and told them she'd decided to go back to Salem. Soon after, as they were shopping, Carrie spotted Mary and managed to detain her while help was called. Unfortunately, Mary had already sold Will on the baby black market. Luckily, French police apprehended the couple who were about to leave the country with Will. Everything seemed to be going well until Paris Children's Protective Services refused to allow Will to leave the country with Sami, an unwed mother.

Once again, Sami ruined what should have been a most happy day for Austin and Carrie. Sami took Carrie's place, in an identical wedding gown, as she became Mrs. Austin Reed. She had no honeymoon, however, as Austin left their suite and sneaked into Carrie's room for some intimate moments. Although Sami had hoped the judge would make them stay longer in Paris, he was convinced the marriage was based on love that would provide Will a stable home and he allowed them to return to Salem immediately.

Vivian and Ivan were in the City of Lights and were stunned to stumble across the duo.

At the same time, Vivian and Ivan were in prison after the ordeal with Stefano. John just wanted his aunt to stay there for a few days, but Kate managed to have Ivan and Vivian's stay extended. With the help of another jailmate, Andre—who knew someone in Salem and was anxious to reach him—the trio escaped.

Andre took off, and Vivian, being chased by Abe, went to the top of the Eiffel Tower and pretended she would jump. The weather turned bad, however, and the wind nearly made her threat real, except that John arrived in time to get her down.

While Peter was spending time with Kristen, Jack and Jennifer bonded and she admitted Jack was much more the man she once fell in love with than the man who divorced her. Together, Jack and Jennifer searched the tunnels for evidence linking Peter to Stefano's illegal businesses. They had no idea Peter had already set explosives to destroy whatever was left of the tunnels. Jack and Jennifer were nearly killed just after Jack saw a ledger with Peter's name on it that would have certainly been the proof he was looking for.

Later, at a Paris casino, Jack managed to lure Daniel into a high-priced poker game. When Daniel couldn't pay his debt, he was forced to tell Jack about Peter's

Paris masquerade ball

A lot of Strauss:

"Roses from the South"

"Treasure"

"Serenade for Strings"

"Tales from the Vienna Woods"

"Blue Danube"

"A Romalei Te Djilas" (Stefano took Marlena out on Bastille Day)

Berlioz's *"Symphonie Fantastique"* (evoked Vivian's past Paris memories)

dirty deals, including his own part in gaslighting Laura, Jennifer's mother. When Jack accused Peter, Jennifer refused to believe him, but Laura told Jennifer that she could at least confirm that Peter was in cahoots with Jude St. Clair. Afterward, Jennifer was devastated and ran out on both Peter and Jack.

Paris held a surprise for Lexie too. After Stefano was assumed dead in the tunnel blast, Lexie learned that Stefano, her father, had left something for her in a safe deposit box. Lexie went to the bank and was given a briefcase, which Celeste and Abe suggested she not open. Lexie eventually did open it and found a video of her father as well as a treasure in jewels.

Soon after, everyone found their way home to Salem.

The Roman Holiday

The Eternal City was the site of love, danger, and intrigue for many months in 1997, as no less than eight Salem residents arrived, each with different agendas.

In May, Bo and Billie were deep into the undercover drug investigation of J. L. King. Bo was anxious for the case to close so he could tell Hope the truth and get their lives back on track. However, things got more complicated.

Hope and Franco were sent to Rome on a modeling assignment. There, Franco confessed his love to Hope and prayed that someday she would feel the same. He promised to be patient. Meanwhile, still on the King case, Bo and Billie also arrived in Rome.

Franco bribed a fortune-teller in Rome to tell Hope that he was the man for her, while Billie tried to convince Bo that they could find happiness together.

J. L. King arranged for "lovers" Bo and Billie to get married in Rome, and when Bo hedged, King suspected Bo was lying. Going through with the wedding was the only way to regain King's confidence. Eventually, the wedding went off as King planned, with Hope as maid of honor and Franco as best man! While Billie felt momentarily victorious, Hope was devastated, and the pain caused her to faint during the ceremony, making things all the harder for Bo.

Billie secretly loved the situation and prayed that Bo would eventually love her again. Bo, to the contrary, simply wished he could soon put an end to the case and get back to Hope. However, when a dirty Interpol agent revealed Bo as an undercover cop, King took Bo and Billie prisoner. Luckily, they made a daring escape.

Meanwhile, Hope was back in Salem, where Abe told Hope the truth about the undercover operation. Hope decided to return to Rome and find Bo; Franco, of course, went with her.

Bo, who had missed his flight, went back to the hotel and found Billie sobbing. She begged Bo for one more night of love. Although they didn't make love, Hope and Franco secretly saw Bo and Billie in each other's arms. Hope was shattered. She and Franco went back to Salem. So did Bo, but Franco managed to keep them apart and one confused about one another. Bo knew that Hope was told about the undercover operation so he was hurt and confused by Hope's rejection.

Back in Rome, Billie was in danger after King's man, Max, found her and intended to do whatever was necessary to keep her from testifying against King, who had been captured and was in prison. When no one heard from Billie, Bo went back to find her. She was already held prisoner by Max and pumped full of drugs. Addicted, no jury would take her testimony seriously. Once she was fully drug-dependent, Max allowed her to walk around Rome and make her scores herself.

Billie tried to fight the urges, but gave in and bought what she needed at Club Fortuna. Bo was stunned when he found Billie, who claimed she wanted to stay in Rome with new friends. While trying to avoid Bo, Billie ran into Max again. While Bo and Max had their confrontation over Billie, she slipped out of the area. Eventually, Bo found Billie and kept her in a hotel room with him. He made Billie call her mom to let her know she was all right. And he then promised to get her through the torture. In fact, the intense situation brought them closer together.

Hotel d'Oro became the center of love, heartbreak, and intrigue for many Salem residents in the summer of 1997.

On the other end of the phone line, to further convince Hope that Bo and Billie were in love, Kate made it sound as if Bo and Billie were enjoying their honeymoon. Next, Kate told Franco, who had been working for her to break up Bo and Hope, to lie low and leave town for a while. So he went back to Italy, and eventually Rome.

After their dramatic and impromptu wedding, Austin surprised Carrie with a wonderful honeymoon in Rome. They enjoyed their lusty holiday to its fullest from the moment they stepped off the plane, shopping, strolling the piazzas,

Carrie and Austin thoroughly enjoyed their honeymoon, unaware of the skilled manipulations being orchestrated around them by an unseen Sami.

dancing, going to a street fair. All the while, they were unaware of the secret plotting around them.

Sami got a job helping Mike in his hospital office. She used the position and proximity to convince him to go to a medical conference in Rome. She even arranged a room at the same hotel where Carrie and Austin were staying. Soon after, Sami hopped a plane herself so she could watch her manipulations, and hatch new plans too.

At a street festival, everyone was wearing masks. Coincidentally, Austin and Mike happened to be wearing the same kind and Carrie mistakenly kissed Mike, setting his heart aflutter. He covered, of course, and the three had a good chuckle.

Sami managed to get a room close to the newlyweds and on more than one occasion spied them making love; once she was even under their bed! She stole Carrie's diary and got some insight into her half-sister's feelings for Mike.

Meanwhile, at the conference, Mike met a former colleague, Debra, and the two took a few days after the conference to see Rome together. Mike admitted to Debra that

Carrie felt the first inklings of jealousy when she saw Mike having a good time with his former colleague, Debra.

Carrie and Austin's honeymoon in Rome

"I Say a Little Prayer"

"You Are So Beautiful"
(haunts Mike and Carrie)

"A Smile Like Yours"
(Mike and Debra dance on rooftop)

"The Music that Makes Me Dance"
(Bo thinks of Hope while dancing with Billie)

"Nobody Knows"
(Sami gets the D.J. to announce "change partners" so Mike and Carrie dance)

---

he was in love with a married woman in Salem and was trying to move on with his life. However, his plans with Debra were blocked at every turn.

Franco was there too and discovered Sami. He threatened to blow her cover if they didn't form an alliance. She agreed. Franco came on to Debra and pointed out that her "boyfriend" seemed to have more interest in that other woman, Carrie. He and Sami also kept Mike and Debra from making love.

Eventually, Bo and Billie ran into Carrie and Austin. To cover for her weight loss and generally run-down appearance, she claimed to have had a bad bout of food poisoning. Later, Bo told Mike the truth and Mike helped with a drug to ease her down. Eventually Austin was told too.

Billie used her crisis and fear that she would have to testify against J. L. King to keep Bo's protection. He had been rejected by Hope so he stayed close to Billie. Eventually, they made love. While Hope was helping John in the jungle, Bo was under the impression that she was on a holiday with Franco. Feeling he had to move on with his own life, Bo pledged himself again to Billie. She was optimistic that their marriage was real.

Sami, Carrie, and Austin ended up on the same flight back to Salem. Sami disguised herself as a nun, but Sister Mary Moira busted her at the airport. She spent a few days working in the convent kitchen doing penance for her deception.

Carrie and Austin started their new home life together; Mike returned to his work without ever making love to Debra. And Franco stayed around to make further trouble and keep close contact with Sami, whom he would need later.

Hopping to Los Angeles

Whether the reason for visiting Los Angeles is an undercover criminal investigation, as it was for Bo and Billie several years earlier; or a medical convention, as it was for Carrie and Mike; or a photo shoot, for Eric and Nicole; the City of Angels has a cherubic Cupid working overtime.

In the summer of 1997, Roman was delivered to Salem unexpectedly—and shockingly—alive. Kristen found out that the ISA agent was the victim of a rare disease. He did not want to come home to die so he had arranged that word of his death would reach Salem, setting everyone free before death actually took him in time.

Kristen convinced Roman that Marlena still loved him and finally persuaded him to come back to Salem. Stefano had plans of his own and was using Roman as his pawn just as Kristen was using Roman in her own game. Kristen delivered Roman to Marlena just before her wedding to John was about to start.

Away from Salem together, both Carrie and Mike saw each other in a new light. Mike was smitten, but Carrie—still in love with Austin—just had fun and if she was aware of any growing feelings, she didn't acknowledge them.

Eric and Nicole are young, attractive, and falling for each other, but their trip to Los Angeles was strictly business. Each had something to prove and success on this first major assignment was a must.

Jay was a bigger secret than the tattoo Nicole kept hidden. Sooner or later the truth about their past relationship was bound to come out.

Stefano allowed himself to be arrested, then went off to the jungle, where the near-mad scientist, Dr. Rolf, would create a cure for Roman. The gift would win Stefano a universal pardon for any and all wrongs he'd ever done to Salem's residents.

Meanwhile, in Salem, Marlena found out about a bacterial diseases conference in Los Angeles and thought of going. Instead, Carrie offered to go so Marlena could stay in Salem with dying Roman. Mike, as a doctor and family friend, joined Carrie.

Being in Los Angeles together was the start of Mike's recognizing his true feelings for Carrie. She was still in love with Austin, who was guilt-ridden over injured Sami and his son, Will. At the hotel, they ended up sharing a suite because of a lost room reservation. One event after another underscored the couple's compatibility and mutual respect.

In a lighthearted moment, Carrie helped Mike one-up an old classmate, Dr. Craig Wesley, by posing as his girlfriend. That scored points for Mike.

Whenever Carrie seemed down over Roman and their inability to find someone with a cure, or the distance growing between herself and Austin, Mike treated her to a night on the town or some similar surprise. The two saw as much of Los Angeles as possible, everything from the beaches to tourist spots like the Hollywood sign, and the mountains beyond.

A few days into the conference, they were given the name of a doctor who might be able to help Roman. He lived in the mountains north of Los Angeles, so the two rented a car and took off in his direction.

Meanwhile, Austin repeatedly tried to reach Carrie, but never left a message. Carrie had called Austin, but Sami erased the tape. Making matters worse, the talkative hotel receptionist commented to Austin that the couple appeared to be having a good time and seemed very much in love. When Austin heard that, he was convinced that he was right, he had been losing Carrie. He had to move on with his life too, and take care of his family. Sure that he no longer had a chance with Carrie, he proposed marriage to Sami and she, of course, accepted.

Meanwhile, as Carrie and Mike headed for the doctor's cabin, there was a storm and the couple had a car accident. Luckily, Mike pulled Carrie from the car before it burst into flames. She was unconscious and cold. In an empty cabin, Mike used body heat to keep Carrie warm in his arms. As she slept with a fever, she dreamed of Austin and innocently and unaware of what she was doing, kissed Mike. He professed his love for her, but she didn't hear. The next day, Carrie was fine, but Mike was in peril when he got bitten by a snake. Carrie saved his life with quick thinking and first-aid skills.

After finally meeting with Dr. Brock, they had a prescription and they were on their way back down the mountain. They hoped the medication would at least make Roman more comfortable. Excited Carrie was anxious to reach people back home and tell them the news.

When Carrie called the Kiriakis mansion, Sami answered and told Carrie that she and Austin were getting married. Carrie was determined to get back to Salem before the ceremony. There were no flights available so she and Mike took a train and did manage to get back to Salem before Sami and Austin were wed.

A year later, Eric and Nicole were assigned to go to Los Angeles together. The duo formed a team: a new fashion photographer for *Bella,* and the magazine's newest face, fledgling model Nicole. The two managed some great shots after Eric got Nicole to loosen up with plenty of beach fun: gymnastics, carousing with Venice Beach musclemen, and simply enjoying each other.

Nicole, secretive about herself and near penniless, was also ambitious, focused, and, it turned out, very fearful of her past coming back to haunt her. It did in Los Angeles.

At first Eric thought a stalker had become infatuated with Nicole. Then after Nicole took off one night by herself, Eric followed her to a seedy part of town and a small, dark bar, where she willingly met with Jay. After nearly coming to full-out blows, Eric turned away from Jay and brought Nicole back to their suite. She told Eric less than a half-truth when she said Jay was a cousin looking for money from her. In fact, Jay was her ex, but she didn't explain that to Eric right away.

The two left Los Angeles after a successful shoot, but Nicole was rightly worried that Jay would turn up in Salem.

New Orleans

Oak Alley

In 1984, New Orleans banker Maxwell Hathaway and his adopted daughter, Megan, arrived in Salem, where he was well-known to corrupt politician Larry Welch, who was actually part of an old Russian spy case.

All kinds of mayhem ensued after Larry forced Hope to marry him, and Megan wanted back her old beau, Bo. Welch accidentally killed Megan. Stefano DiMera needed three prisms that would cure his otherwise fatal illness. The heist of the prism from a New Orleans art show, and the Welch wedding reception, brought Bo and Hope to New Orleans for the first time.

While Bo's private investigator buddy, Howie, lost the prism to a bayou alligator for a while, Bo and Hope found some stolen moments for romance. They made love for the first time at the Oak Alley Plantation after they pledged their love in an exchange of vows witnessed only by God. It would be another year before the pair could officially wed.

Maison Blanche

A decade later, in spring of 1994, one of Stefano DiMera's many hideaways turned out to be in the New Orleans area too. When Kristen decided to use the old plantation-style house as a grand site for a charity benefit ball, many of Salem's residents enthusiastically packed their bags.

Maison Blanche held many secrets, which Kristen, hoping only to secure the house as an historical landmark, knew nothing about. These included a dungeon where John had been held captive in the past and was taken again by Stefano. There was a mysterious specter of a woman roaming the many old halls. She looked incredibly like Hope, but her name was Gina.

Here Stefano's longtime companion and confidante, exotic psychic Celeste, was first introduced. She quickly developed a jealous hatred of Marlena. And she kept Kristen drugged so she wouldn't find Stefano in hiding, or Marlena, or John chained in the dungeon.

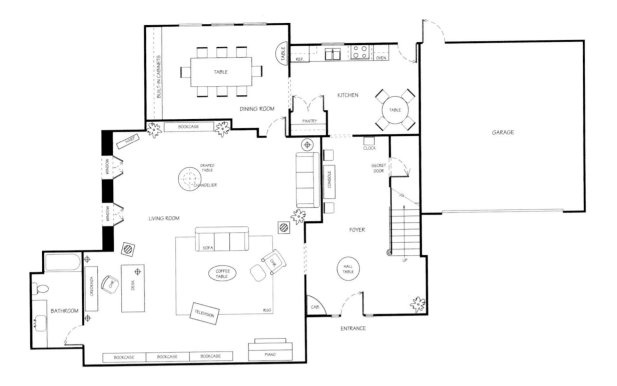

MAISON BLANCHE

Somehow, the charity ball went along beautifully. Peter proposed to Jennifer at a charming inn. However, shortly thereafter, Kristen discovered Stefano was still alive; Roman rescued Marlena and John from the house set afire by Celeste; Tony was temporarily blinded; and Gina, looking so much like Hope's clone, was dumped at Bo's feet a heartbeat after he proposed to Billie at the inn. Stefano again escaped.

John Black realized he had been held prisoner in the same dungeon when he found words he had scratched into the wall. Marlena did everything she could, including trying to seduce Stefano, to get the key to John's cell.

The Bayou

Oddly enough, it was John and Hope's trek into the jungle and another of Stefano's secret hideouts that led Hope back to New Orleans. Dr. Rolf, who was concocting the potion to make Roman well, recognized Hope. Later, in Stefano's locked room, Hope's memory was jogged by other hints that took her senses back to Maison Blanche. Back in Salem again, it was Stefano's art books and photos in the basement of "Jonesy's" town house that further stirred Hope's vague thoughts about her lost years. Stefano had found Hope after she was horribly scarred and disfigured by acid. He claimed that her numerous surgical procedures and recuperations took many years in hospitals and at Maison Blanche in recovery. Hope, however, had nagging doubts about how she had spent her time during that period. She remembered nothing, but was determined to piece together clues, bit by bit, until she could puzzle out the missing years of her life.

Celeste gave Hope an ornate antique comb and brush set that was once hers, as well as a compact engraved with the letter *G* for Gina, as she was called in her Maison Blanche days. Hope traveled to New Orleans–area hospitals to talk to other doctors who had worked on her. Slowly, stray threads started coming together. It would take months before a pattern could emerge. The deeper Hope delved, the more far-reaching her search became, sending her to Switzerland too.

Checking out her past, Hope visited New Orleans and its bayou, unaware of the secrets and dangers hidden within.

When the Swamp Girl first saw Hope, she had an immediate affinity for her. The two shared secrets and pieces of the past together, but it would take Hope a long time to uncover them all with Bo's help.

Meanwhile, the bayou held further intrigue and mystery. A frightened Swamp Girl became fascinated by Hope, and by her *G*-engraved compact, which she stole as Hope slept.

Later, pregnant Billie went into the bayou in search of Bo, who was trying to help Hope. While there, Billie delivered a stillborn child, a daughter she named Georgia because one of the boys in the cabin where she birthed had played that tune on his guitar. When Billie found a compact in the bayou with a letter *G* on it, she took it as a sign that her Georgia would always be with her in spirit. Back in Salem, Billie hid the true details of her bayou birthing and blamed her miscarriage on Hope after the two had a confrontation. She even carried out a funeral and led Bo to believe the baby was in the coffin.

Bo, convinced that the mysterious Swamp Girl knew something about Hope's past, searched her out and befriended her. Bo and Hope's past, from the first time they made love at Oak Alley, has been linked to New Orleans and its deep dark bayou.

Pregnant Billie had hoped to find Bo and bring him back to Salem with her, but she prematurely went into labor. More determined than ever to hold Bo, Billie kept the secret of how and when she miscarried in order to manipulate both Bo and Hope.

The Jungle Adventure

Stefano was betting on the ace up his sleeve when he allowed himself to be arrested in Salem. When he earlier helped Kristen bring deadly ill Roman back to Salem, he had begun to put a plan into action. He knew he had the cure to make Roman well again and found a way to turn it into a bargaining chip. Once arrested, Stefano promised the cure to save Roman's life. In return, Stefano would have full pardon on all his past offenses. He'd be a free man in Salem for the first time, allowed to own and operate businesses, and have a public social life too.

All Stefano had to do was be released so he could get the cure from his secret laboratory deep in the jungle. His willing return would show that his word was, indeed, good. No fool, John decided to go with him to make sure Stefano returned. Kristen went too, hoping for some time with John to maybe win him back; Hope hopped aboard the plane as John's partner and to protect Marlena's interest against Kristen's moves.

At the jungle compound, John and Hope were sometimes held in confinement—especially after wandering about and discovering Stefano's secret shrine-to-

Marlena room and a doctor who recognized Hope. That encounter left Hope with the nagging notion that there was more to her past than she could remember about Maison Blanche, and a determination to find out more.

Stefano did have a cure, but he fumbled the vial and it was lost. In order to concoct a new batch, a rare flower had to be plucked from the jungle full of hostile natives and a variety of natural obstacles. When there were no volunteers from the compound, John offered to go. Hope was told to stay behind, but she joined him anyway.

In their quest, the two encountered natives with bad attitudes, rock slides, fires, tarantulas, and plenty of unseen, dangerous stalking critters. More than once the two had to climb, swim, run, and hide for safety. Eventually, they spotted the special orchid. As they reached it, the natives reached them. Stefano's helicopter pilot tossed a smoke bomb and plucked Hope away from harm. John had the flower but was clubbed by a native and was presumed dead when he didn't return to the compound in feasible time.

When the natives attacked the compound, Stefano and his last remaining cohorts prepared to leave. Stefano was not happy. Without the flower, there was no cure; without the cure, there was no pardon and all of Stefano's plans would be ruined. Hope railed at a very worried Stefano that he would spend the rest of his life in jail. Stefano did not care if John was alive or dead, but needed to get the flower that might still be in John's backpack, so he sent his native employees into the jungle. They returned with John's watch, and nothing more. Eventually, John escaped the hanging cage where he was held. After a few more dangers and delays, the troupe managed to leave the jungle.

Of course, there was another obstacle. Their plane went down. Still, they got back to Salem—and just in time to keep Marlena from remarrying Roman in the hospital chapel. The cure was made. Stefano was free. Roman was cured.

Stefano's compound was a maze of rooms and chambers holding all sorts of secrets. This one was a shrine to Marlena with her photos and varied memorabilia. For a time it also held the precious cure for Roman. When the vial was accidentally dropped, the real adventure began.

John with a case of jungle madness? No, he's swatting a big, poisonous tarantula off Hope's shoulder blade. Luckily, he has good aim!

Romantic and Dangerous Getaways

Salem residents travel near and far, often at a moment's notice. Some of the most romantic, most dangerous, or most exciting getaways are not too far from home.

Green Mountain Ski Lodge

A favorite spot for Carrie and Austin, it's an easy few hours' drive north of Salem. It was here that they first made love in Room 114.

Shortly thereafter, Alan Harris, a military school buddy of Lucas, donned a ski mask and tried to rape Carrie. Thankfully, he failed. A few years later, after Carrie and Austin hit some rough times, Carrie came back to the lodge with Lucas. She was hoping to move on emotionally. At the same time, Sami was in Salem trying to seduce Austin, but Bo returned with Hope and everyone changed their plans and celebrated together in Salem.

Then in summer of 1996, Carrie and Austin recognized the truth of Sami's plots against them and how she had drugged Austin to get him into bed with her. They came back to their romantic retreat to make new memories.

Of course, Sami didn't give up. Later that year she followed the couple to the resort, put her sister's negligee on, and crawled into their bed, where she waited for Austin. When Carrie found her there, the two got into a fight and Sami had the nerve to press charges and have Carrie arrested.

Lucas was still interested in Carrie and joined forces with Sami. He arranged for Mike to go here when Carrie was waiting for Austin. By the time Austin showed up, Mike and Carrie were in a hot tub together and Austin felt some serious fears about losing her. The doubts plagued him for quite some time and made it easier for Sami to work her schemes.

Summit Lake

This is another favorite getaway spot, more private than the lodge. Carrie and Austin, and Lucas too, have enjoyed times at a mountaintop cabin on Lakeview Road.

Salem Airport

This international facility offers direct flights to Paris, England, Aremid, and most any other place any Salem resident wants to go. And if there are no commercial flights, there are a number of private planes for hire, or owned by the DiMera, Kiriakis, and Alamain families.

In 1996, Stefano found out from Kristen which flight Marlena and Rachel Blake would be on. When John found out that Stefano was in Salem, he stopped the plane and, when it was searched, found a fake mustache and captain's outfit on the floor inside. He foiled one kidnap attempt, but Stefano's next plan, with Kristen's help, worked just fine. Stefano stole Marlena away and made it appear that the plane they were on exploded in the air. Soon John figured out the ploy and eventually realized, from clues in a board game found at the DiMera mansion, that Stefano likely took Marlena to Paris. He hopped his own private jet and tracked Stefano down and saved Marlena.

As one of the most logical exits from Salem, the airport had been the site of other drama too. Checking some flight logs, Jack realized that Peter had ordered the DiMera jet ready to take off at a moment's notice and realized that Peter's plan to kidnap Jennifer and Abby was being put into action. However, he couldn't con-

Whether flying commercial or by private jet as Stefano and Kristen always do, the Salem International Airport is a full-service air transport facility.

vince authorities that anything was going to happen and took matters into his own hands, stopping Peter himself back at the house. With Peter shot and Jack arrested, no one was flying anywhere.

Once Kristen managed to convince John to elope, she got him as far as the airport. They were about to board John's plane when Marlena showed up and, unaware that Kristen had already miscarried, reminded Kristen that flying would endanger her pregnancy. Kristen had to continue her pregnancy ploy and the elopement came to a halt.

Keeping people from leaving sometimes works and sometimes doesn't. When Billie wanted to go back to Europe, Hope convinced her not to go until the romantic triangle—Billie, Bo, Hope—was settled. Billie stayed, but the triangle continued to shift and turn at different angles.

When Hope and Marlena tried to stop John from going on his jungle trek with Stefano to find a cure for Roman, they couldn't convince him, so Hope secretly joined him by hiding on Stefano's plane until they were in flight.

In late 1997, Sister Mary Moira caught Sami, disguised as a nun, coming through customs from Rome.

A few weeks later, John and Marlena sent Susan and her baby, Elvis, off to somewhere Stefano wouldn't find them. After Susan was gone, the couple thought they had complete privacy on John's plane. They didn't realize that Kristen had sent Roman to the plane, setting everyone up for disclosure. Roman watched as Marlena and John kissed and talked of their future together, and their guilt over lying to Roman. After they left, an enraged Roman trashed the cabin.

It was at the airport, in early 1998, that Abe and Roman stopped Susan from leaving the country after they found out Kristen had apparently drowned in her swimming pool. Of course, Kristen was alive and well, disguised as Susan, whom she had sent off into white slavery.

Eventually, Susan escaped her captives, and Kristen and Edmund—on John's plane—had their face-off. Edmund and Susan got the upper hand and flew to England with baby Elvis after having Kristen picked up and shipped off to the eccentric sexy slave master in the Caribbean.

Cayman Islands

It was no fun-and-sun vacation for Jack and Jennifer when they flew to the islands to investigate a bank account that could link Peter and Jude to illegal activities. Posing as a couple, the two signed up as bank teller trainees to gain access to the bank's computers.

While Jack and Jennifer were at the bank, Jude called to try and gain access to the account Peter had set up for him. When Jack finally got the chance to examine the account records in the computer, he saw that the account did, indeed, belong to Peter. Unfortunately Peter, almost simultaneously, learned what Jack was up to and managed to wipe his name off the account. Only Jack saw his name and Jennifer refused to believe Jack. Peter also tipped the bank officials off and Jack and Jennifer were forced to make a hasty return to Aremid.

Somewhere at Sea

After Kate Roberts' plane went down because Vivian had drugged the pilot's coffee, Kate was presumed dead. However, a fishing vessel had plucked her from the ocean and saved her. Unfortunately, it would not be going to port for six months and the captain was not willing to make special arrangements to have her lifted off.

Eventually, she convinced a crewman to help her escape, but the plan was interrupted and the best she could do

It was no glamorous sea cruise for Kate, who was thought dead but was actually adrift and earning her way on a commercial fishing vessel.

was to jump overboard. She got herself to a small island, where she met a helpful man named Zip and his wife, Helena, who lived there. They were not in completely primitive surroundings. In fact, they had a television and Kate caught a news segment featuring Vivian with Victor as they celebrated Kate Roberts' memory with the opening of a new pediatric wing at the hospital.

Kate vowed to make it back to Salem and decided to brave the ocean in a crudely constructed raft. It got her as far as another island, where a pilot finally agreed to help her get back to Salem.

New York

In early 1996, Carrie and Lucas took a short business trip to New York and grew momentarily closer as friends. Upon returning to Salem, Austin was about to tell Carrie he still loved her. But when he saw Carrie with Lucas he thought they were actually dating, and so he said nothing.

Santa Rosa

This charming vacation spot is off the beaten track for tourists but still offers full amenities, including plenty of peace and quiet for honeymoon couples. It's where Bo and Hope spent their first honeymoon, in the Room of Eternal Love.

Sadly, it also became the place where Bo and Hope were able to obtain a quickie divorce when he kept his promise to marry Billie. He had fallen in love with Billie and proposed, before Gina, who was actually Hope, was returned to Salem.

A master of setting up situations, Franco busted the pipes in a Santa Rosa hotel room so he and Hope had to share a room; and Bo found them together.

Much later, Franco and Hope were assigned to go to Santa Rosa for a modeling job for Secrets perfume to appear in *Bella Magazine*. After a night of fun and the Mexican hat dance, Franco managed to flood his room so he had to share a room, and bed, with Hope. Ironically, it was the Room of Eternal Love. When Bo came to Santa Rosa to surprise Hope, he found Hope and Franco in bed together.

When they returned to Salem, Hope was offered a modeling contract. Taking it as she did caused further distance between Bo and Hope at a time when they could have been reconciling their differences and finding new romance. Franco, however, had been secretly hired by Kate to keep the two apart.

England

With the help of Marlena and John, Susan was able to get her baby boy, Elvis, out of Kristen's clutches. They sent the mother and child off on John's private jet to a place where neither Stefano nor Kristen would think to search. They set up housekeeping in a cozy cottage in a small town in England.

There, Susan met Violet the innkeeper and her son, Edmund, who was nearly as eccentric as Susan. They also shared a huge interest in Elvis Presley songs and memorabilia. Susan and Edmund enjoyed a sweet courtship with a simple picnic in the countryside and a variety of oddball antics that set their hearts in tune. About the time it was clear Edmund and Susan were in love, Stefano's henchman Bart came snooping around. Violet sent him off on another track.

Soon Susan was unexpectedly visited by Vivian, Ivan, and Jonesy from Salem. As fate would have it, Jonesy was originally from that very same town in England. He and Vivian honeymooned at a quaint bed-and-breakfast across the road. Unfortunately, Jonesy didn't survive his wedding night, and Vivian inherited his Salem town house filled with all his worldly goods. He never told her that they were not his but in a kind of informal trust for Stefano, who simply didn't want his name on any property in Salem.

Susan made one mistake. She faxed a newspaper clipping about Vivian's wedding with her own photo in it to Marlena. Unfortunately, Kristen had been snooping around the penthouse and found the fax, a clear clue to Susan's location. It also alerted another Banks quadruplet.

While Edmund was away in London, Susan got a mysterious phone call, then another from Kristen saying that she had Sister Mary held hostage and demanded Elvis as ransom. Kristen forced Susan to agree to come to the States with Elvis. She even indicated exactly what she was to wear.

Edmund's poem to
Susan 1/24/98:

She flew into the village
This peculiar bird
Distinct in her look,
Even more so in her word.
And there was I,
Alone, praying for love
Heaven has answered
On the wings of a dove.

It was on John's private jet that Edmund confessed to killing "Kristen"
in the Blake House pool. It was there that he and Susan wed before
leaving Salem.

Susan Banks was set up in a quaint English cottage by John. There she met her eventual husband, the unlikely
romantic hero, Edmund Crumb.

Beyond Salem   185

Edmund's promise to Susan:

I promise our days will be filled with sunshine, our nights with the light of a million stars. Our hearts and souls will now be one, and we'll soar together on the wings of love until our days on this earth are done.

Edmund's proposal to Susan:

Susan,

You have given life to my heart, renewed my soul with faith and joy. The light of your sweet goodness and beauty shines still after evening falls. To live life without you is to feel the cold wind of loneliness. Marry me, my precious Susan, and I will pledge to you my heart, my soul, my body, and my motorscooter too.

Within a short time of Susan's return to Salem, Kristen was found dead in her pool—or at least that's what most people believed. In fact, Susan had been sold into slavery, and Kristen portrayed Susan in order to get Elvis.

Susan was first carted off to an Arab land, where she did her best to belly dance for a sex-crazed fantasy freak. She failed the test and would have been killed if she hadn't saved him from choking. The more-than-eccentric mystery man then took his traveling companions to a Caribbean island, where he gathered still more women to his encampment. Susan managed, after several attempts, to escape.

Eventually, Edmund came to Salem and surprised Susan with a wedding. Later, he explained to "Susan" that he accidentally killed Kristen—who turned out to be Penelope, the fourth Banks quad. The real Susan, meanwhile, managed to return to Salem and got to Edmund, Kristen, and Elvis before they took off in John's jet for Bermuda for their honeymoon. Susan turned the tables on Kristen and had her taken to the Caribbean camp. She then explained to Edmund he was better off keeping the secret of his part in Penelope's death. The two wed on the plane and took off.

Susan and Edmund returned with Elvis to England to start their own life together. But first, Susan contacted Stefano and, pretending to be Kristen, told him that she, Elvis, and Edmund were going on an extended holiday. She would be in touch at some later time.

On the Lam

After Travis/Trent kidnapped Jennifer, Jack broke out of jail to rescue her before she was handed over to Peter. His quest took him to a remote cabin in the Grand Canyon where Travis fell to his death. Jack rescued Jennifer and they returned to Salem. Jack was still not a free man. Until he could prove Peter was alive, he was on the lam. Jennifer and Abby stowed away in his car and went off with him.

It turned into a most unusual family adventure when the trio joined Ward's World-Famous Circus traveling through Columbus, Ohio. Peter caught up with them when the circus came to Salem. Luckily after Jennifer was thought to be dead—but was alive and fulfilling an angelic fantasy—Peter was caught and Jack was freed. All the travel of the last few months must have sparked a wanderlust in the couple. They packed their bags and the trio went to South Africa to visit Jennifer's dad, Bill Horton, and reestablish their family relationship in another environment.

Part Six

Salem Lifestyle

Churches and Parks

St. Luke's Roman Catholic Church

This is the parish of the Brady family and part of many important events in their lives and those of other Salem residents.

Weddings, baptisms, and funerals have been performed here. Salem residents have found moments of peace and serenity, counsel and comfort as they prayed. Among the weddings here: Marlena and Roman (1986), Kimberly and Shane (1987), Adrienne and Justin (1990), John and Isabella (1992), Tony and Kristen (1994), Bo and Billie (1995), and Carrie and Austin (1997).

During Christmas Mass in 1993, baby Belle, kidnapped by her half-sister Sami, was returned unharmed. At her baptism about a month later, Marlena confessed having an affair with another man.

By the end of 1994, the Desecrator (devil-possessed Marlena) took a hammer to knock off the heads of three saintly statues in the church that she would later

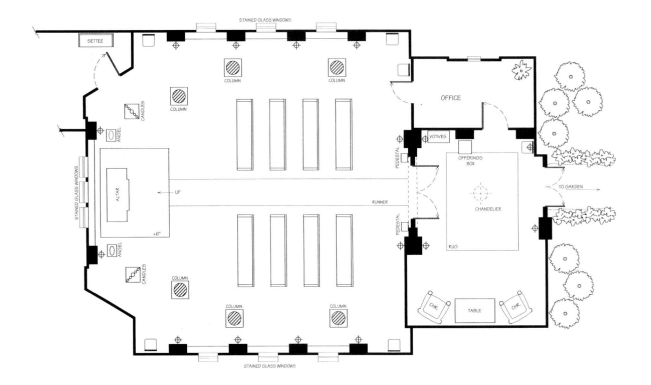

ST. LUKE'S CHURCH

try to burn down. Kristen was also attacked, stripped bare, and painted with pentagrams while handcuffed to the altar rail.

In July 1995, Sami put a halt to Carrie and Austin's wedding by announcing she was pregnant with his child.

It was here too, after Peter's funeral services, that Laura discovered Kristen was only padded, not pregnant, and that both Peter and Stefano were alive. That information proved very dangerous to her. They hauled her off to a secret room in the Blake house, where a laser procedure made her forget.

Early in 1997, Kristen confessed just about all her sins to Father Jensen and then wanted him to perform a surprise wedding between her and John. The priest strongly suggested that Kristen come clean with John and Marlena first.

In May, a heartbreaking memorial service was held for Roman, who was reported dead on an ISA mission. Within a few months, however, during John and Marlena's preceremony preparations, Roman was returned to the same church, very much alive. Before the bride made her entrance, Kristen delivered an ailing Roman to the anteroom, bringing the wedding to an end before it started.

When John discovered through Stefano's computer records that he was a Roman Catholic priest, he did what he could do to honor his vows until he finally obtained the appropriate Church writ removing his obligation.

During Peter's funeral, Stefano—who had been thought killed below the streets of Paris—was very much alive. He hid in the church confessional and listened to the memorial for Peter, who was also still alive!

Only a few months later, Sami's summer wedding to Austin became quite a dramatic event when Carrie and Eric, with Mike's help, stopped the already once interrupted ceremony to lay bare more of Sami's secrets, including Will's true paternity. Carrie also decked Sami so hard she was out cold on the church vestibule floor. Within a very short time, Carrie and Austin's long overdue wedding commenced while family and guests were still gathered.

During Kristen's funeral in early 1998, less than grief-stricken attendees listened to Stefano's eulogy become an enraged attack on them. He got so worked up, he had a heart attack and would have died had not Lexie jumped into action and saved his life.

Glory Day Protestant Church

Another church was the scene of drama when Jennifer's memorial service held more than one surprise. Peter, in the throes of jungle madness, showed up toting an automatic rifle and was met not only by Stefano and law enforcement among those gathered, but a hovering Jennifer in angel form. Peter's gun was real, the angelic vision was not. Jennifer was really alive after all.

Sami's wedding to Austin was halted and Carrie ended up being the bride that day. Others, like Jennifer and her mom, Laura, were preoccupied with other matters: Jennifer worried about imprisoned Jack, and was angry that Stefano would not admit Peter was still alive, as Laura insisted. If Peter were known to be alive, Jack would be freed of his murder sentence.

St. Monica's Convent

Unvisited until Susan Banks' sibling, Sister Mary Moira, came to Salem, this convent became a place of refuge for some and penance for others.

When Vivian and Ivan almost kidnapped Sister Mary, thinking she was Susan in nun disguise, Sister Mary decided her own brand of punishment would be more fitting than anything the authorities would deliver. She had the duo scrub convent floors.

Doling penance turned out to be her forte. When Sister Mary came across Sami disguised as a nun at the airport returning from Rome, Sami did her penance by serving the convent full of nuns their meals and handling kitchen duty.

Disguised as Susan, Kristen managed to fool Sister Mary and retrieved baby Elvis from the convent after manipulating a drugged Susan into signing custody papers.

After Sister Mary Moira discovered a delirious Celeste, she allowed her to rest at the convent. Likewise, Laura found refuge here when the court, thinking she had a part in Kristen's murder, considered shipping her back to a psychiatric facility.

Laura was terrified that she would be sent back to the sanitarium in the aftermath of Kristen's death and Laura's belligerent behavior. Celeste suggested she spend some time with Sister Mary Moira at St. Monica's Convent. Meanwhile, worried family and friends searched frantically.

The Cemetery

This is one of a number of local burial places and mortuaries.

Before Jennifer could have the body properly exhumed and tested, Kristen made Ivan dig up Daniel's body in Peter's grave and had it cremated.

In February of 1998, because Stefano missed Kristen's burial when he had a heart attack during the funeral service, he went to the cemetery and visited her grave. While talking aloud, Kristen—disguised as Susan—overheard him. She revealed herself as alive and asked for his help. She kept up the charade and planned to get baby Elvis and leave Salem.

While Carrie and Austin drew closer, Sami and Lucas met to discuss devious plans to come between the romantic couple. What better place to conspire than during a holiday fest in the park?

When Eric came upon Madison, a teenage runaway, he helped her find her way, gave her a Bible, and sent her back home from the Salem bus station.

Or what better place among greenery, flowers, and friends in good spirits to propose? Carrie accepted (again) and they made their own plans.

Parks

Salem residents make good use of their local parks for community picnics, parades, and concerts. Individually and as couples, they enjoy taking a leisurely stroll or finding a quiet bench to sit upon as they contemplate their woes or plan their future.

Sometimes, as was the case with John, an unlikely homeless man named Gabe turns out to be an angel.

Unfortunately, the day Jennifer sat down to think about her troubles, it was only Stefano lurking in the area.

Peter discovered Stefano in the park and wanted to turn him in to the police, until Stefano promised to help Peter get Jennifer and Kristen get John.

In summer 1997, Marlena and John were in the park and thought someone was eavesdropping on them from the bushes. John reached for the fellow, but before he could deck him, they realized it was Eric, who had finally returned from Denver.

<table>
<tr><td>

Titan picnic '95

"After Hours"

"Only Wanna Be with You"

"Bad Reputation"

"Evie's Tears"

"Sleeping Satellite"

"Did You Know It Was Me?"

</td></tr>
</table>

During the Horton-Brady picnic—while Billie lashed out at Hope and Sami and Franco announced their engagement—married woman Carrie and Mike exchanged an impulsive kiss in a moment of excitement over their victory in the Chief of Staff campaign and their long-simmering attraction.

Salem's Most Memorable Weddings

In Salem, being engaged, walking down the aisle, and sometimes even exchanging vows is no guarantee that a true marriage has taken place. Still, romantic couples, and a few conniving ones, keep trying!

Every wedding holds hope and sometimes offers trials of love.

Carrie Brady and Austin Reed

JULY 27, 1995 • ST. LUKE'S R.C. CHURCH

The wedding party included Carrie's half-sister, Sami, as maid of honor. Lucas was best man and the bridesmaids included Carrie's stepmom, Marlena, friends Wendy and Gina—who was not yet confirmed to be Hope—and about-to-be sister-in-law Billie. The women in the wedding party wore light purple dresses with tiny beading around the shoulders and bustline.

Carrie's wedding gown with a cathedral-length train was made of white silk satin with a reembroidered lace edge on the skirt. The lace, used for the sheer sleeves and over the bodice too, was sewn with pearls and sequins. A tiara-style headpiece was covered in pearls and an illusion veil with lace trim was attached. A lace-trimmed satin bow adorned the back of the gown at the waist.

As part of the wedding ceremony, Austin recited a poem to Carrie:

I love you. Not just for who you are,
but for who I am when I'm with you. I love you.
Not for what you've done with your life . . .
but for what you're doing to mine.
I love you for making me good . . . and happy. And whole.
Because that is what you do, Carrie.
Without a word. Without a gesture. Without a doubt.
Just by being yourself. Such a simple thing . . .
but no one else in the world could do it.
Only you.

Unfortunately, in the midst of an otherwise romantic and long-awaited wedding, Sami became faint. The nuptials were interrupted when Sami announced she was pregnant with the groom's child and put an end to what should have been Carrie's happiest day.

Picture-perfect bride Carrie is ready to marry the only man she ever loved.

John, then a priest, was happy to perform the ceremony.

Carrie Brady and Austin Reed

SEPTEMBER 8, 1997 • ST. LUKE'S R.C. CHURCH

Likely the best impromptu wedding in Salem history, it started with the planned wedding of Sami and Austin. However, as delays multiplied, Carrie and Eric became determined to expose Sami's schemes. Eric told Roman that he had doubts about what was happening, and Roman pretended to faint to buy some time. Meanwhile, Eric and Carrie went to University Hospital to find information on what Sami was hiding. With Mike's help, they discovered that Austin wasn't Will's father at all. Carrie returned to the church in time to stop Austin from making a big mistake.

After Sami's lies were dramatically revealed and Carrie laid her out cold with a powerful punch, Austin proposed to Carrie and guests had a wedding ceremony after all. Luckily, Austin and Carrie's marriage license was valid for one day more.

Carrie wore the dress she had worn on her failed wedding day in 1995.

The ceremony was short and sweet, and went off without any problems, other than Sami's screaming through the window, trying to stop the ceremony. The best man was a reluctant Mike Horton, who was still fighing his love for Carrie.

Marlena was the matron of honor and Abby Deveraux was the flower girl. While everyone was scurrying to pull the wedding together, John bought wedding rings for the couple to exchange.

The reception was held at the Kiriakis mansion as had been planned. Sami, still in her wedding gown, created a memorable moment when she crashed the party and caught the bridal bouquet. Still, everyone else had a wonderful time. The bride and groom danced to their song, "I Only Have Eyes for You." Among other special songs for this couple, and played at various times during their reception: "For You I Will," "Love Me Tender," "There's No Easy Way," "The Color of My Love," and "Suddenly."

Carrie and Austin spent their wedding night at the Salem Inn (with plenty of interruptions from Sami) before leaving for their honeymoon in Rome. Their lusty holiday was a dream come true for the couple, unaware of Sami's prying presence until after they returned to Salem.

Carrie and Austin's wedding reception

"I Love You Always Forever"
(first dance as husband and wife)

"I Only Have Eyes for You"

"Butterfly Kisses"

"I Only Have Eyes for You"
(when they later make love)

Sami Brady and Austin Reed

SEPTEMBER 24, 1996 • PARIS, FRANCE

With heartbroken Carrie as maid of honor, Sami and Austin wed in order to bring back Will to the United States. Will had been kidnapped by Sami's neighbor, Mary, who had sold the tyke on the black market to a childless couple in Europe.

Mary, Will, and investigators from Salem crossed paths with Carrie and Austin, who were in France on holiday and planning their own elopement wedding. Austin, who at that point still thought he was Will's father, really had no choice but to marry Sami since it meant the child could be brought home to Salem rather than remain in French social workers' care. A judge had refused to release the baby to anything less than a stable two-parent family.

Sami bought a dress at Madeline's, a Paris shop where Carrie had bought hers. Sami also chose the exact same dress Carrie had selected.

While an instrumental "Pavane" played, Sami gloated and glowed as she made her vows. Austin, far less enthusiastic, mouthed the words that made him Sami's husband, as shattered Carrie witnessed the wedding that should, again, have been hers.

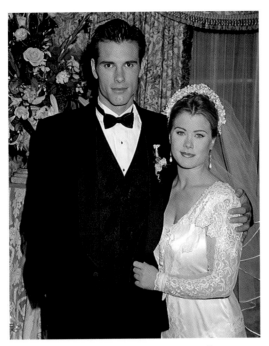

The second time Sami stole the groom from Carrie, she wore the same dress Carrie had chosen!

There was no honeymoon for the couple, but Sami did try her best to seduce Austin on their wedding night. He, however, would have nothing to do with her, even if, in name, she was his wife.

The marriage was annulled in fall of that year, 1997, but not before Austin again went through the vows for Sami's sake at the Salem hospital. She had lain unconscious and near death after he accidentally ran her down with his car. Only the tape of their Paris wedding, and hearing the "Pavane" again, stirred her back to life.

Shortly after, because Sami suffered amnesia and needed reassurance that would speed her recovery, Austin and Sami spoke the renewal wedding vows:

Austin: I, Austin, take you, Samantha, to be my wife. I promise to love, honor, and cherish you, in sickness and in health, in good times and in bad. I will love you all the days of my life.

Sami: I, Samantha, take you, Austin, to be my lawfully wedded husband. To have and to hold from this day forward, in good times and in bad, in sickness and in health, to love, honor, and cherish all the days of my life.

Austin: With this ring I pledge my love.

The moment was one of Sami's few innocent victories.

Sami Brady and Austin Reed

SEPTEMBER 8, 1997 • ST. LUKE'S R.C. CHURCH

After Sami convinced Austin that it would be in Will's best interest if they wed for real, Austin proposed to Sami even though he had finally gotten their Paris wedding annulled and was free to marry Carrie. Austin was ready to let Carrie go because several people in Salem, including Sami, of course, had convinced him that Carrie would be better off with someone like Dr. Mike Horton.

⌒ℳℳ⌒

**Austin and Sami's wedding,
Salem '97**

Boccherini's "Minuette" Op. 13,
No. 5 (Austin and Lucas wait for
Sami at the altar)

"Trumpet Voluntary"
(Roman and Sami embrace, walk
down the aisle)

"Bridal March"
(Sami notices no one looks happy)

⌒ℳℳ⌒

Looking her loveliest ever, Sami was riding a victory high as her dad, Roman, was about to give her away to Austin.

The wedding was planned and everyone was assembled at the church. Lucas Roberts was the best man and Marlena was the matron of honor. Roman, of course, still recuperating from his mystery illness, was thrilled to be giving away his daughter at the wedding she had planned for so long. Ironically, he and Eric would join forces to put a stop to the nuptials in enough time for Carrie to do some last-minute investigating.

Even during the delays, Sami looked radiant (although perhaps a bit nervously flushed) as she waited for the ceremony to resume. Sami wore her hair in cornrow twists that became a bun in the back. Her white wedding gown had a low-cut bodice.

Carrie hauled off on Sami with a slug and knocked Sami out cold! By the time she woke, no one believed her lies.

The ceremony eventually resumed, but Carrie rushed into the church just before Austin said "I do," and put a stop to the vows. Carrie had proof that Sami had been conniving through her amnesia and, furthermore, she had proof that Will was Lucas' son, not Austin's.

Bo Brady and Billie Reed

JANUARY, 1995 • ST. LUKE'S R.C. CHURCH

The bridesmaids, Carrie, Gina, Kristen, and Jennifer, wore off-the-shoulder long dresses that were a dark orange-yellow. Billie and Jennifer hired Jacque Marcell, a designer from Europe, to make them.

Billie's wedding gown had an off-the-shoulder lace bodice with a satin skirt. The bodice was also covered with rhinestones. The back of the skirt, which carried a cathedral train, had a satin bow. There was a lace appliqué on the train of the skirt, which was a different lace from the bodice. Her headpiece bore fabric flowers and pearls in a tiara shape with a lovely sparkle-illusion cathedral-length veil.

The wedding rite came to a very unceremonious halt when the chandelier above the couple suddenly crashed down, barely missing them. It was the handiwork of the devil, who had, by then, possessed Marlena.

> **Bo and Billie's wedding reception '95**
>
> "True Companion"
> (first dance as husband and wife)
>
> "Girl with the Indigo Eyes"
>
> "The Lights Went Out"
>
> "Look at Us Now"
> (they make love)

That interruption, as dramatic as it was, was not the move that stopped the wedding. Stunning the churchful of friends and family even further, kindly Alice Horton actually voiced her objections to the vows. She was still convinced that Gina was really Hope, and therefore, any vows Bo would make would be invalid, the marriage bogus and completely unfair to her granddaughter. At that point, the priest could not be convinced to marry the couple, since it was possible that Hope was alive, and Bo would then still be legally married.

Bo Brady and Billie Reed

FEBRUARY 24, 1995 • ST. LUKE'S R.C. CHURCH

This time around, Hope/Gina was not part of the wedding party. Her identity as Hope had been accepted and she and Bo divorced to clear the way for him to marry Billie.

Bo and Billie's wedding vows:

Bo: I, Bo, take you, Billie, to be my wife to have and to hold forever. They say that love is the light that lights the world and that kindness paves the road to happiness. You and I have traveled kind of a long and winding road, you know. On a snowy mountainside we pledged our love and our faith and our fidelity to each other. We felt God's presence that night just like we feel God's presence tonight in this rebuilt church. I promise to love and to honor and to cherish you all the rest of the days of our lives.

Billie: I, Billie, take you, Bo, to be my husband to have and to hold forever. The road that we traveled has had some despair, but our love and our faith that we were meant to be together lighted our way. I will not only be a wife to you, but I will be your friend and I will be your soul mate. I'll share your sadness and your sorrows as well as your happiness. I promise to love, honor, and cherish you for all the days of our lives.

There were plenty of white roses, Billie's favorite, often given to her by Bo during their courtship.

Billie added a simple gold band next to her engagement ring, which was a diamond with a ruby on one side of it and a blue topaz on the other. Bo had commented when he gave it to her, ". . . a one-of-a-kind ring for a one-of-a-kind love."

At their reception, there was no falling chandelier, but to everyone's shock, Marlena arrived naked.

Bo Brady and Billie Reed Brady

JUNE 16, 1997 • ROME, ITALY

Not quite literally a shotgun wedding, it came close. Drug dealer J. L. King arranged everything for Bo and Billie. It was another test of their loyalty to him and proof that they weren't lying to him all along. Of course, they had been. They had been thrown together through the course of Bo's undercover investigation and would do nothing to make King suspect they were working for the police.

King sent a "mystery" wedding invitation to Hope and Franco, who were staying at the same hotel, Hotel D'Oro, while doing a fashion photo assignment. At first, Hope thought the stylist for the shoot was getting married and was shocked to discover that it was Billie and Bo. To further the irony, Billie's wedding gown was the same one that Hope had worn for the fashion layout just the previous day. And although Hope and Franco arrived as the invited guests, they became the official witnesses.

Bo tried, to the last minute, to stop the wedding, but there was no way out. Billie, who understood the whole situation was, nevertheless, delighted. Hope, on

The strain showed on Hope's face when she found herself the maid of honor at Bo and Billie's wedding in Rome.

the other hand, was so overcome by the events that she fainted during the exchange of vows. She came around and encouraged them to continue while Bo was silently wishing it was Hope he was marrying that day. As he kissed his bride, Billie, he thought only of his wedding to Hope in England many years back.

At the reception immediately following the tense ceremony, Bo and Hope danced to "His Is the Only Music That Makes Me Dance." During that time in each other's arms, Bo wanted to tell Hope how he felt and the truth of the situation, but he just could not risk the operation or endanger everyone present.

Bo and Billie remained in Rome as the drug operation came to a dramatic close. There was no honeymoon. The couple consummated their marriage only after several months passed. During that time Bo went back to Salem and was rejected by Hope, then returned to Rome to find Billie hooked on drugs. He helped her through a torturous withdrawal, and the experience brought them together again. They made love and Billie conceived a child.

Bo Brady and Hope Williams

MAY 23, 1985 • ST. MARY'S CHURCH, THE COTSWOLDS, ENGLAND

In appreciation for saving the life of a royal, Lady Joanna, and capturing the Dragon, a magnificent wedding was provided by the Lady's family.

On the morning of her wedding day, Hope wrote a letter to Bo, which she put inside the puzzle box given to her by her grandfather Tom Horton.

The wedding party consisted of the maid of honor, Melissa Anderson, and bridesmaids Marlena and Kimberly; the best man was Howie Hofstedder; the groomsmen were Abe and Shane. Carrie was the flower girl and Tom Horton walked his granddaughter down the aisle.

As friends and family arrived from Salem for the ceremony, Bo and Hope were detained for debriefing. Bo, who was running even later, missed the limo so he stole a milk wagon to get to the church. He was arrested. Then, in handcuffs, he borrowed a horse and got to the church with no time to spare. Shane got the cuffs off and he showered and changed at the church.

The cathedral was laden with tons of flowers. A full choir sang Beethoven's "Ode to Joy" as they entered and filled the sanctuary. Then Howie escorted Alice down the aisle; followed by Shawn and Caroline; then

Early Bo and Hope

"Just Once"
(Hope ice-skating, 1985)

"The Greatest Affair" (Hope's wedding to Larry Welch; Liz sang but Hope thought only of Bo)

"Star Crossed"
(Hope's London fantasy)

"Love Between Us"
(Bo sang it to Hope during their wedding)

"When I Fall in Love"

"Your Warm and Tender Love" (during Hope's premonition of losing Bo on the Cruise 1990)

"Star Crossed"
(Bo-Hope fantasy in London 1985)

"Just Once" (Hope ice-skating with flashbacks 1985)

Bo; Shane and Kimberly; Melissa; and finally Hope on Tom's arm.

At the altar, the music changed and Bo personally serenaded his beloved "fancy face" with the song "Love Between Us."

They exchanged traditional vows, and the minister proceeded with the double ring ceremony after reminding them: "The exchange of rings is a custom that dates back to the early days in Rome when rings were made of gold coin. Men would give them to their wives as a symbol that they were willing to share with their wives all their worldly possessions. Today, the ring is made of gold that can never tarnish. As a perfect circle, it symbolizes the love that has no beginning and has no end."

Bo repeated the ring ceremony words: "With this ring, I thee wed. With my body, I thee honor, and all my worldly goods with thee I share. Amen."

Then Bo added his own words as he looked into Hope's glowing face:

"Hope, I know it's taken us a long time to get here. I'm sure there were times

Bo and Hope's wedding in 1985 still remains the most glamorous and moving of any Salem residents'. It was literally fit for a royal pair!

you thought that we wouldn't; I know I had my doubts. I never thought that I could have someone in my life who could make me so happy, make me feel so alive. You know how hard it is for me to tell people how I feel about them, especially the people I care about. But today, in front of all these people, I have no problem telling you that I love you. I want you to know that, and I want them to know too.

"Like the Archbishop said, I know our lives are not going to be all sunshine and roses from here on in, but I want you to know, I'll try my hardest to keep our love alive because we've got something very special here—worth fighting for. I love you, Hope."

After Hope repeated the ring ceremony, she added her own words too:

"I guess I fell in love with you the first time I saw you. But it's taken me all this time to realize that what I felt, then, was nothing compared to what I feel now. Remember what we said to each other in New Orleans? 'True love is the gift that God hath given to man alone beneath the heavens; the silver link, the silver tie, which heart to heart and mind to mind, in body and in soul can bind.' I was pretty young when you met me and I get so mad at you when you call me Little One. But knowing you and loving you has made me grow into a woman. And I am your woman, Bo. Standing here in front of all these people, I give you my life and all my love for now and all eternity. Oh Bo, I love you! And I'm so proud to be your wife."

Hope's wedding gown was a Paris original, handsewn and beaded. It was made of twenty yards of tissue-weight silk satin for the bodice and skirt. Thirty yards of silk illusion tulle was used for the veil, yoke, sleeves, and overskirt; added to that were fifteen yards of silk hand-embroidered lace with French sequins and pearls. The bodice had a high embroidered lace neck that gave way to the sheer illusion yoke and sleeves. The drop-shoulder line of the bodice was encrusted with flowers cut from lace, wired to be dimensional, and beaded with crystal and pearl centers. The back of the bodice was sensually sheer, closing with four dozen tiny satin buttons. The sleeves were also sheer with embroidered lace at the wrists, each closing with an additional dozen buttons. The figure-skimming bodice was sculpted of silk satin ending in a snug drop waist.

The three-layered skirt with its sweeping ten-foot train was comprised of a bottom layer of silk satin and two overlayers of illusion tulle. The top layer of the tulle was trimmed with the hand-beaded embroidered lace, and the circumference of the hem was a dozen yards long.

The headpiece was based on a scalloped cap that encircled the bride's head. Rising from the cap was a coronet of beaded lace flowers and a swath of gathered tulle reflecting the new French look. The veil was three graduated layers of tulle, the longest of which was ten feet long, blending with the train.

Bo wore a designer ankle-length rider's coat, wing-collar shirt, and black crushed velvet vest.

The bridesmaids wore peach satin and chiffon gowns highlighted with sequins; the maid of honor wore a lavender version of the gown.

The happy couple missed their own reception because Emma, under the escaped Dragon's hypnosis, attempted to kill Bo and Hope when the final music, "God Save the Queen," was played. Shane saw her enter the church and saved the couple, who then took off in a royal carriage.

The honeymoon got off to a rough start too. Bo and Hope were arrested in their hotel room as Bo was about to carry Hope over the threshold. They spent their wedding night in adjoining jail cells because of the stolen milk wagon incident.

Bo Brady and Hope Williams Brady

NOVEMBER 11, 1996 • ST. LUKE'S R.C. CHURCH

The prewedding party at the Horton house was filled with tension because the Billie-Bo-Hope triangle had not been totally resolved. Bo worried obsessively about Billie and her safety since she was hanging out with Franco, whom Bo believed had attacked several women in Salem. Hope took his concern for love, an assumption that Franco encouraged because he had been hired by Kate to break up the couple so Billie could have a chance to be with Bo again.

At the party, guests enjoyed champagne and cake that had been topped with two lovebirds. Melissa, Kimberly, Marie, dad Doug, and Hope's half-sister and step-mom, Julie, also arrived in Salem for the nuptials.

The wedding party included: Jennifer as the maid of honor; bridesmaids Lexie, Wendy, and Sami paired with Austin. The women wore long fuschia gowns. Hope had asked Carrie to be in the wedding party, but Sami got a restraining order against Carrie, who then was not allowed to attend the party at the Horton house or set foot in the church, anywhere near Sami.

Hope's gown had a bodice of reembroidered satin with a flower design and one-inch straps. The back laced up with organza ribbon. A full silk organza skirt with three layers was trimmed with quarter-inch satin ribbon. The headpiece was made of satin ribbon with handmade roses and an illusion veil to fingertip length.

Hope put together the traditional good-luck charms. She borrowed a lace handkerchief, had a new diamond pendant necklace, wore a blue garter, and had an old boat compass. However, there was not good luck enough to make this wedding happen.

Bo had gone to Smith Island looking for Billie because he feared for her safety with Franco—who had gone off with her so she would not be alone in her pain as Bo married another woman. Bo found her and she convinced Bo that everything

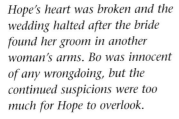

Hope's heart was broken and the wedding halted after the bride found her groom in another woman's arms. Bo was innocent of any wrongdoing, but the continued suspicions were too much for Hope to overlook.

Salem Lifestyle 209

was all right. However, when Bo tried to leave the island, he discovered his boat was out of gas, then missing; the radio was out of order and there were no phones on the island. A passing helicopter failed to see him signal for help. Bo even tried to swim back to the mainland but didn't have the strength. Exhausted, back on the island shore, Billie took him to the cabin. There, Billie stripped off his wet clothes and let him sleep, with her body around him for added warmth. And that's how Hope and Franco found the duo when she arrived, still wearing her wedding dress. Hope accepted no excuses. The wedding was off.

Bo Brady and Carly Manning

DECEMBER 10, 1991 • ON TOP OF A PYRAMID IN CHICHÉN ITZÁ, MEXICO

With Marlena, Isabella, Roman, and John as witnesses, Bo and Carly exchanged informal but very personal vows even though she was still married to Victor Kiriakis.

They wore traditional Mayan wedding garments. Bo placed a necklace with a north star pendant around Carly's neck. Then Carly recited a poem to Bo:

I know not if the voice of man can reach to the sky
I know not if the gods will hear as I pray
I know not if the gifts I asked for will be granted
I know not what will come to pass in our future days
I hope that only good will come, my love, to you.
(Carly put a jade ring on Bo's finger.)
I know now that the voice of man can reach to the sky
I know now that the gods have heard as I prayed
I know now that the gifts I asked for have all been granted
I know now that the word of old we truly have heard
I know now that our future days will have no number
I know that only good will come, my love, to us.

Bo went on to tell Carly how he would be honored to be her husband. She responded that he has brought her heaven on earth and the only thing that could make it better would be to be his wife. And they continued their exchange of promises.

Bo: I, Bo, take you, Carly, to be my wife, my love, and the mother of our children. I will be yours in good times, and in bad, in sickness, and in health, in failure, and in triumph. I will cherish you and respect you, comfort you and encourage you, today and for the rest of our lives.

Carly: I, Carly, take you, Bo, to be my husband, my love, and the father of our children. I will be yours in good times, and in bad, in sickness, and in health, in failure, and in triumph. I will cherish you, and respect you, comfort you and encourage you, today and for the rest of our lives.

Everyone enjoyed an informal reception at the home of a local anthropology professor, and Bo and Carly spent their wedding night in a native hut-style room.

Bo Brady and Carly Manning

DECEMBER 11, 1992 • ST. LUKE'S R.C. CHURCH

This time, in a formal setting with more friends and family present, Bo and Carly intended to make their earlier vows valid with a traditional ceremony.

Jennifer was matron of honor and Roman was best man; John and Marcus were ushers, and Shawn-Douglas was the ring bearer.

Carly's gown had a 1940s look in off-white, four-ply silk with a short puddle train. The off-shoulder bodice had long sleeves and a layer of reembroidered appliqué lace over silk. Small wax flowers were used for the headpiece.

Midway through the ceremony, Carly's ex-beau, Lawrence Alamain, burst into the church. He announced to everyone present that Nikki, previously thought to be the adopted charge of Vivian, was really his son by Carly. The emergency of the moment was that Vivian had kidnapped the boy and neither was anywhere to be found. All this was news to the groom, who was too shocked to say very much as the bride went off to find her son. The wedding was not continued at a later date.

Jennifer Horton and Peter Blake

NOVEMBER 11, 1995 • AREMID

Mom Laura was matron of honor, Tony was the best man, bridesmaids were Kristen and Hope, and Bo and Mike were groomsmen.

The wedding ceremony took place in spite of Jack's continued attempts to make Jennifer change her mind. Minutes before the wedding, Jack climbed through a window to reach her as she got ready. After literally slapping him away, Jennifer married Peter.

The bride's gown was a copy of the one in the portrait found at the Aremid Blake house. It was the one Peter's mother had worn. The figure-skimming bodice of silk satin was highlighted with a bodice drape and soft lace sleeves; it was trimmed with silk flowers in soft pink. The skirt, also in silk satin, had a soft lace apron trimmed with pearl fringe. There was a satin bustle at the back of the skirt over a lace inset down the back center of the skirt. Pearls and sequins sprinkled the reembroidered lace. A sparkle-illusion veil of fingertip length was held in place by a simple comb.

It was almost six months later before the couple embarked on a world-tour honeymoon. They got as far as England and Paris before Peter's past was finally uncovered by Jack and Daniel Scott.

Jennifer and Peter's wedding reception

"Sentimental Reasons"
(first song as husband and wife)

"Blues in Hoss's Flat"

"At Last"

"Moonlight Serenade"

Jennifer Horton and Jack Deveraux

JULY 2, 1991 • WILD WEST ARENA

It was a year to the day that the couple first made love during the Cruise of Deception.

Carly was maid of honor, and Marcus stood in for Jack's brother, Steve, as best man. Jennifer's dad, Bill, walked her down the aisle; her mom, Laura, was released from the sanitarium for the day. There were almost four thousand people at the public event.

Jennifer's gown was a simple princess-line sheath of Swiss cotton lace hand-beaded with crystal bugle beads and seed pearls. The underskirt was soft pink silk satin. Soft pink satin flowers, with aurora borealis lochrosen and small net fabric butterflies with pearls were sewn to the shoulder area. The neckline was trimmed with baroque pearls with scattered lochrosen over the bodice and the sleeves. A five-yard silk satin train with a Watteau-style back was gathered, fanlike, at the shoulders. There were more fabric flowers and butterflies where the train dropped off the back.

Jennifer's halo-style headpiece was made of soft pink satin gathered and studded with aurora borealis lochrosen. Three fabric roses and butterflies with bugle beads were attached to the base. Three layers of sparkle-illusion net created the short veil.

The bride's "something old" was the blue garter grandmother Alice wore when she married Tom. The groom was considered the "new," and something borrowed came from Carly. She had saved Jennifer's first pair of studded earrings that Jennifer wore continually after getting her ears pierced. At the time she promised to save them for Jennifer's wedding day.

The overflowing reception was held at a riverfront restaurant, the Sand Dollar. The couple enjoyed their honeymoon in Hollywood, California.

Jack's wedding letter to Jennifer:

Dear Jennifer,

From the day we met, you've surprised me, challenged me, and engaged me in a way that no other human being ever has. And I've never been able to tell you what that meant to me. But today of all days I have to find a way.

Before I knew you, I wasn't living. I was waiting, and hoping, because even though I've lived my life in a gray and soulless city, I've always known that in the heart of it there was a wall and there was a door. And if you're lucky enough to find the key and lucky enough to find your way, we'll be about as close as any of us is ever going to get to the Garden of Eden. And I know this is going to sound ridiculous, but standing here with you, it feels like that's exactly where I am, sans the snakes and the apple trees, of course.

Then Jennifer recited:

Now we will feel no rain
For each of us will be shelter to the other.
And now we will feel no cold
For each of us will be warmth to the other.
Now there is no loneliness
We are two bodies,
but there is one life before us and one home.
When evening falls, I'll look to you
and there you'll be.
And I'll take your hand and you'll take mine
And we'll turn together and we'll look to the road
we traveled to reach this—
The hour of our happiness.
It stretched far behind us,
and our future lies ahead—
A long and winding road
where every turning means discovery
All the hopes, new laughter, shared tears,
The adventure has just begun.

John Black and Isabella Toscano

MAY 19, 1992 • ST. LUKE'S R.C. CHURCH

Shawn walked the very pregnant bride down the aisle. Carly was the maid of honor, and Bo was best man.

Isabella gave birth to the couple's son, Brady Victor Black, before the marriage vows were completed. After delivering the baby in an anteroom, she was wheeled back to the sanctuary and the couple completed their vows while Isabella held the child in her arms. When John was told he could kiss the bride, she and the baby were sound asleep.

Kristen Blake and Tony DiMera

FEBRUARY 18, 1994 • ST. LUKE'S R.C. CHURCH

Kristen's floor-length wedding gown was well-fitted and made of lace reembroidered with pearls and lochrosen. Silk organza attached at the waist extended to create a ten-foot train. Two organza bows at each shoulder point added detail to the bodice, highlighted with a six-strand pearl choker at the neck. Fabric flowers crowned the fingertip illusion veil.

The couple's first wedding ceremony was interrupted when Belle was kidnapped and Kristen wanted to help John find the child.

On the final wedding day, John tried to stop Kristen from marrying Tony, but Stefano told Kristen John was Belle's father. When Stefano tried to make his getaway, John shot after the car, it exploded, and, more out of guilt than love, Kristen married Tony as Stefano would have wished. It turned out to be another Stefano ploy.

John Black and Susan Banks, posing as Kristen

JUNE 23, 1997 • DIMERA MANSION

Everyone was dressed in Elvis-era style. Susan, who looked like an odd cross between herself, Kristen, and Priscilla Presley, wore a heavily sequined and pearl-studded gown. Her hair was high and her eyeshadow blue. John was shirtless

Susan really thought she had succeeded in getting John to marry her. The zany wedding was no more valid than the first time John married "Kristen" in the hospital delivery room as she (Susan) gave birth to John Jr./Elvis.

under a leather jacket and pants. Abe wore a leather jacket, gold shirt, and a Colonel Parker–type cowboy hat. Matron of honor Vivian and Ivan, an usher, were also dressed in the style of that time.

During this wacky wedding, Marlena and Kristen were trying to break through a wall in the secret room, and Stefano was disguised as a waiter, hoping to make off with Marlena. The women broke a gas line and were left unconscious.

Meanwhile, during the reception upstairs, Laura came rushing in and demanded that Kristen confess to all her manipulations. Everyone thought Laura was crazy until the false teeth Susan used as part of her disguise flew out of her mouth when Laura shoved her. Susan admitted she had both Kristen and Marlena locked in the secret room. They were freed just in time or would have died of the gas fumes.

> **John and "Kristen's" wedding '97**
>
> "Blue Suede Shoes"
> (starts the event)
>
> "True Love"
> (Ivan walks bride down the aisle)
>
> "I Married Her Just Because
> She Looks Like You"
> (reception)

When Marlena came around, she recounted all of Kristen's lies and secrets for everyone to hear. Kristen did not give up; she tried to convince John to marry her on the spot anyway. He would not.

Roman Brady and Marlena Evans

FEBRUARY 9, 1983 • ST. LUKE'S R.C. CHURCH

For their wedding poem they chose Johann Wolfgang von Goethe's "True Season of Love":

That is the true season of love
When we believe that we alone can love
When no one has ever loved so before us
And no one will ever love in the same way after us.

The preparations and ceremony were disrupted by constant attempts on Roman's life. Marlena even spent the wedding night in the protective care of Don Craig in disguise while Roman continued his underground police work against Stefano.

Marlena Evans and Roman Brady (John)

AUGUST 22, 1986 • ST. LUKE'S R.C. CHURCH

Maggie was matron of honor, with bridesmaids Kimberly and Kayla. Abe was best man, and Chris and Shane the groomsmen. Carrie was the flower girl, and Eric and Sami also joined the procession. The ceremony took place just days after Marlena recovered from a month-long coma she had suffered from a fall off a window ledge where she had talked down a suicidal patient.

Marlena to Roman: I love you. I got you back. You have no idea what that means to me, Roman. I believe that to have someone come into your life whom you love as fully and completely as I love you is rare, and special, and something to be cherished. And, oh, how I cherished what we had. When you were gone I held on to that feeling we had, and even though the pain from missing you was unbearable, I felt lucky for having had what we did. Some people never find it. But we got a chance to have it twice in a lifetime. And I know what it's like to be without you, for a day, for a month—actually, for seventeen months, three weeks, and two days. That's how long I hurt, and my heart ached to be with you. But all of that just makes this time, what happens from this moment on, all the more special. We're more than lucky. We're more than blessed. We've been twice blessed. I love you . . . I love you.

Roman to Marlena: Doc, circumstances have kinda dealt us a funny hand and there are things from my life, which includes our life, that I don't remember. But I remember the first time I saw you, after I came back again. You were in the hos-

It was the groom, not the bride, in this wedding who had an identity crisis that even he didn't know about. Brainwashed by Stefano, John returned to Salem in a way that everyone would accept him—as presumed-dead Roman.

pital, working. I had no idea about anything from my past. But there was still a connection; my heart stopped.

You can take a human being and do a lot of things to him, but you cannot take away his love. I love you. It is that simple. A lot of the people here might have thought that all that time you were in the hospital, lying in that bed, I might have thought I was going to lose you, or that I'd already lost you. I didn't. I couldn't lose you. You're my life. Sweetheart, you're my reason to get up in the morning, to lay down at night. But you know what I would do? Every day, I would talk to you. I would watch your children grow, looking for some evidence of you in them. And I would cry, for what we were missing. We were meant for each other, Marlena. I'm just so happy that we found each other. I love you.

Marlena Evans and John Black

JULY 18, 1997 • ST. LUKE'S R.C. CHURCH

The wedding party included Carrie, Laura, Lexie, Abe, Belle, and Brady. Marlena chose a short, pale yellow dress, with a hood-style veil.

This wedding was stopped before it began. Kristen brought dying Roman, who had already been presumed dead, into the church's anteroom, where Marlena was getting ready. There was no way either Marlena or John could continue the ceremony.

At last! Marlena was all set to marry John since he got his identity straight, and both were free of other loves.

Three Strikes, You're Out!

Kate Roberts and Victor Kiriakis

SEPTEMBER 6, 1993 • PENTHOUSE GRILLE

It was a simple ceremony with Marlena Evans as matron of honor and John Black as best man. Although the couple had real affection for each other, it appeared to be a marriage of convenience, more of a business merger than a blissful wedding. The ceremony was quick, the vows were to the point, and no one knew at the time that the marriage was invalid anyway. Kate herself did not know she was still married to her first husband, lowlife Curtis Reed.

Afterward, there was a small reception at the site, the Penthouse Grille.

Vivian Alamain and Victor Kiriakis

JANUARY 19, 1995 • KIRIAKIS MANSION

Sixteen months late, it turned out Victor and Kate were really in love. They had survived the turmoil of discovering that Curtis Reed had been alive at the time of the last Kiriakis vows. That made their first vows invalid, but Curtis's murder cleared the way for a real marriage. As Kate and Victor were immersed in too many other activities, Vivian took charge of all the wedding plans and arranged a surprise rehearsal for Victor and Kate. She knew that Kate would be occupied elsewhere and obligingly took Kate's place during the run-through. Vivian slyly turned the rehearsal into a valid exchange of vows without the groom ever guessing the truth.

Kate Roberts and Victor Kiriakis

FEBRUARY, 1995

Given Vivian's hijinks of the month prior, this exchange of vows would not have made Kate Mrs. Kiriakis anyway. Still, the timing of Vivian's next surprise roadblock could not have been more perfect. Vivian went into labor and gave birth to the couple's child, Phillip. The rarely outwitted Alamain had stolen the couple's in vitro embryo, carried the child full-term, and delivered the child as their wedding gift . . . their "almost" wedding! It wasn't until September that Victor learned he was actually wed to Vivian.

Salem's First Really Wacky Wedding Outfit

Calliope Jones and Eugene Bradford

DECEMBER 31, 1985 • UNIVERSITY PARK

Marlena was best "man," Anna was maid of honor, and Carrie was flower girl. Calliope wore a dress covered with white Christmas lights that lit up as she walked down the aisle to the tune, "When You Wish Upon a Star."

The groom wore a white fur coat.

After the vows, there was a reception at the Salem Inn and the couple took their honeymoon in Finland.

Cast List and Credits

ERIC	Eric Roman Brady	Jensen Ackles
HOPE	Hope Alice Williams Welch Brady	Kristian Alfonso
BILLIE	Billie Holliday Reed Brady	Krista Allen-Moritt
LAURA	Laura Ann Spencer Horton	Jamie Lyn Bauer
BRADY	Brady Victor Black	Eric/Brandon Billings
CELESTE	Celeste Perault	Tanya Boyd
WILL	William Robert Brady Roberts	Shawn/Taylor Carpenter
CARRIE	Caroline Anna Brady Reed	Christie Clark
MICKEY	Michael Horton	John Clarke
MIKE	Michael William Horton	Roark Critchlow
NANCY	Nancy Wesley	Patrika Darbo
LUCAS	Lucas (Horton) Roberts	Bryan Dattilo
TAYLOR	Taylor Raines	Katherine Ellis
IVAN	Ivan Marais	Ivan G'Vera
MARLENA	Marlena Evans Craig Brady Bradford Brady	Deidre Hall

JOHN	John (Forrest Alamain) Black	Drake Hogestyn
LEXIE	Alexandra (Perault/DiMera) Brooks Carver	Renee Jones
KATE	Kate Elizabeth Winograd Reed Roberts Kiriakis	Lauren Koslow
ALI	Ali McIntyre	Lisa Linde
LILI	Lili Faversham	Millicent Martin
STEFANO	Stefano DiMera	Joseph Mascolo
GRETA	Greta	Julianne Morris
SHAWN-D	Shawn-Douglas Brady	Collin O'Donnell
SHAWN	Shawn Brady	Frank Parker
AUSTIN	Austin Reed	Austin Peck
BO	Beauregard Aurelius (Kiriakis) Brady	Peter Reckell
ALICE	Alice Grayson Horton	Frances Reid
ABE	Abraham Carver	James Reynolds
MAGGIE	Maggie Simmons Horton	Suzanne Rogers
VIVIAN	Vivian Alamain	Louise Sorel
CRAIG	Craig Wesley	Kevin Spirtas
SAMI	Samantha Gene Brady Reed	Alison Sweeney
ROMAN	Roman Augustus Brady	Josh Taylor
CAROLINE	Caroline Brady	Peggy McCay
ROLF	Dr. Rolf	Will Utay
NICOLE	Nicole Walker	Arianne Zuker

Long Crawl Credits

(Current *Days of our Lives* staff)

Executive Producer
KEN CORDAY

Executive Producer
TOM LANGAN

Supervising Producer
STEPHEN WYMAN

Producer
SHERYL HARMON

Directed by
HERB STEIN
PHIL SOGARD
RANDY J. ROBBINS
ROGER INMAN

Written by
SALLY SUSSMAN MORINA

DOROTHY ANN PURSER
MARLENE CLARK POULTER
DENA HIGLEY
VICTOR GIALANELLA
MEREDITH POST
PETER BRASH
PEGGY SCHIBI

MARALYN THOMA
BRUCE NECKELS
JOYCE ROSENBLAD
and
FRAN MYERS

Senior Coordinating Producers
JEANNE HANEY
JANET SPELLMAN-RIDER

Coordinating Producer
TOM WALKER

Cast:
Starring
FRANCES REID
as
Alice Horton

Mickey Horton
    JOHN CLARKE
Maggie Horton
    SUZANNE ROGERS
John Black
    DRAKE HOGESTYN
Caroline Brady
    PEGGY McCAY
Shawn Brady
    FRANK PARKER
Abe Carver
    JAMES REYNOLDS
Vivian Alamain
    LOUISE SOREL
Carrie Reed
    CHRISTIE CLARK
Samantha Brady
    ALISON SWEENEY
Lexie Carver
    RENEE JONES
Lucas Roberts
    BRYAN R. DATTILO
Ivan Marais
    IVAN G'VERA
Laura Horton
    JAMIE LYN BAUER
Mike Horton
    ROARK CRITCHLOW
Hope Brady
    KRISTIAN ALFONSO
Celeste Perrault
    TANYA BOYD
Austin Reed
    AUSTIN PECK
Bo Brady
    PETER RECKELL

Shawn-Douglas Brady
    COLLIN O'DONNELL
Kate Roberts
    LAUREN KOSLOW
Billie Reed
    KRISTA ALLEN-MORITT
Stefano DiMera
    JOSEPH MASCOLO
Roman Brady
    JOSH TAYLOR
Eric Brady
    JENSEN ACKLES
Nicole Walker
    ARIANNE ZUKER
Craig Wesley
    KEVIN SPIRTAS
Greta
    JULIANNE MORRIS
Ali McIntyre
    LISA LINDE
Nancy Wesley
    PATRIKA DARBO
Taylor
    KATHERINE ELLIS
Lili Faversham
    MILLICENT MARTIN

with DEIDRE HALL
as
Marlena Evans

Theme by
CHARLES ALBERTINE
TOMMY BOYCE
BOBBY HART

Music Composed by
KEN CORDAY
D. BRENT NELSON

Music Directors
AMY BURKHARD
STEVE REINHARDT

Production Designer
DAN OLEXIEWICZ

Associate Directors
ROGER W. INMAN
MASON DICKSON

Production Associates
DAVID N. KOHN
DEBBIE WARE BARROWS
JULIE BRADY

Production Manager
TIM STEVENS

Property Master
TOM TROUT

Special Effects
PETE TRZEPACZ

Art Director
TOM EARLY

Assistant Art Directors
STEVE NIBBE
SHEREE MILLER
NIKI MUNROE

Assistants to the Producers
NANCY LEWIS
TERRY ANN HOLST
STUART W. HOWARD
TERRI LYNN DOUBET
SUZANNE RAY

Continuity Coordinator
DARRELL RAY THOMAS, JR.

Writers' Assistants
CHER ANN BOGGS
ANDREA ARCHER
CYDNEY KELLEY

Publicist
DAVID SPERBER

Stage Managers
FRANCESCA BELLINI DeSIMONE
JOSEPH LUMER

Casting by
FRAN F. BASCOM, C.S.A

Associate Casting Director
LINDA POINDEXTER

Casting Assistant
RONALD SPERBER
RICK LORENTZ

Costume Design
RICHARD BLOORE

Wardrobe
SHERRELL CONEO
JIM PFANNER
CONNIE SECH
KELLY KNUTZEN
GEORGE COOPER
DONNA OBERMAN

Makeup Artists
GAIL HOPKINS
NINA WELLS
GAIL BRUBAKER
JOLEEN RIZZO
CORINA DURAN

Hairstylists
ROD ORTEGA
GARRY ALLEN
FABRIZIO SANGES

Technical Director
J. C. O'NEILL

Lighting Directors
DON DeSIMONE
TED POLMANSKI

Audio
DAVID CONE

Boom Operators
RALPH CRUSE
BRUCE BOTTONE

Senior Video
BILL GARDHOUSE

Video Tape Editors
MASON DICKSON
BRUCE BRINKERHOFF

Cameras
JOHN SIZEMORE
MIKE CARUSO
MIKE MECARTEA

Sound Effects
TOM KAFKA

Electronic Maintenance
LORENZO M. SEPULVEDA
RON HANFF

Executive in Charge of
Production
GREG MENG

Senior Executive in Charge of
Production
GARY FOGEL

A
CORDAY
PRODUCTIONS, INC.
PRESENTATION
Copyright 1999

Photography and Art Credits

Photographs

Page

ix	*left*, Corday Productions/Patrick Chisholm
ix	*right*, CBS Photo
xvi	JPI/John Paschal
6	JPI/John Paschal
11	JPI/Betsy Annis
12	*upper*, JPI/Betsy Annis
12	*lower*, JPI/Betsy Annis
14	JPI/John Paschal
15	Corday Productions/Ken Bank
17	Corday Productions/Ken Bank
18	Corday Productions/Ken Bank
20	*top left*, Celebrity Photo/John Paschal
20	*center*, Celebrity Photo/John Paschal
20	*bottom left*, Celebrity Photo/John Paschal
22	NBC/Gary Null
23	NBC
26	*upper*, Celebrity Photo/John Paschal
26	*bottom*, Celebrity Photo/John Paschal
27	NBC
28	NBC
32	NBC
36	JPI/John Paschal
37	JPI/John Paschal
38	*right*, JPI/John Paschal
38	*left*, JPI/John Paschal
43	Lesley Bohm
46	JPI/John Paschal
47	JPI/John Paschal
48	JPI/John Paschal
50	JPI/John Paschal
52	JPI/John Paschal
53	*top*, JPI/John Paschal
53	*bottom*, JPI/John Paschal
55	*left*, NBC/Alice S. Hall
55	*right*, NBC/Alice S. Hall
56	Corday Productions/Ken Bank
60	*top left*, JPI/John Paschal
60	*bottom right*, JPI/John Paschal
62	Charles Bush
63	JPI/John Paschal
65	NBC
66	NBC/Dave Bjerke
68	JPI/John Paschal
70	JPI/John Paschal
71	JPI/Aaron Montgomery
72	NBC/Chris Haston
74	NBC/Dave Bjerke
76	JPI/John Paschal
82	*top*, JPI/John Paschal
82	*bottom*, NBC/Gary Null
85	*top left*, JPI/John Paschal
85	*middle*, JPI/John Paschal
85	*middle left*, JPI/Betsy Annis
85	*bottom*, JPI/John Paschal
87	Dana Fineman
88	NBC
91	Jonathan Exley
92	Robert Sebree
94	JPI/John Paschal
95	NBC
96	NBC/Chris Haston
96	JPI/John Paschal
97	JPI/John Paschal
98	*left*, JPI/John Paschal
98	*right*, JPI/John Paschal
98	*bottom*, JPI/John Paschal
99	JPI/John Paschal
100	JPI/John Paschal
105	*top*, JPI/John Paschal
105	*bottom*, JPI/John Paschal
106	JPI/John Paschal
107	JPI/John Paschal
109	JPI/John Paschal
111	*top*, NBC/Paul Drinkwater
111	*middle*, Hutchins Photo Agency
111	*bottom*, JPI/Aaron Montgomery
113	*left*, JPI/John Paschal
113	*right*, JPI/John Paschal
113	*bottom*, JPI/Aaron Montgomery
115	JPI/Aaron Montgomery
117	*left*, JPI/Aaron Montgomery

117   *right,* JPI/Aaron Montgomery
117   *bottom,* JPI/Aaron Montgomery
118   JPI/Aaron Montgomery
119   JPI/Aaron Montgomery
122   *top,* JPI/John Paschal
122   *bottom,* JPI/John Paschal
123   JPI/John Paschal
125   *top,* JPI/John Paschal
125   *middle,* JPI/John Paschal
125   *bottom,* JPI/John Paschal
128   *top,* NBC/Alice S. Hall
128   *middle right,* Hutchins Photo Agency
128   *middle left,* Hutchins Photo Agency
128   *bottom,* JPI/John Paschal
129   *top,* JPI/Aaron Montgomery
129   *bottom,* JPI/Aaron Montgomery
131   Celebrity Photo/John Paschal
132   Celebrity Photo/John Paschal
136   *top left,* Celebrity Photo/John Paschal
136   *top right,* Celebrity Photo/John Paschal
136   *bottom right,* NBC/Gary Null
136   *bottom left,* Celebrity Photo/John Paschal
137   *top,* JPI/John Paschal
137   *middle,* JPI/John Paschal
137   *bottom,* JPI/John Paschal
138   *top left,* JPI/John Paschal
138   *top right,* JPI/John Paschal
138   *middle,* JPI/Betsy Annan
138   *bottom,* JPI/Aaron Montgomery
152   Hutchins Photo Agency
156   *top,* Celebrity Photo/John Paschal
156   *middle,* Celebrity Photo/John Paschal
156   *bottom,* Celebrity Photo/John Paschal
162   JPI/John Paschal
163   *top,* JPI/John Paschal
163   *bottom left,* JPI/Aaron Montgomery
163   *bottom right,* Celebrity Photo/John Paschal
164   Celebrity Photo/John Paschal
165   Celebrity Photo/John Paschal
166   *top,* Celebrity Photo/John Paschal
166   *middle,* Celebrity Photo/John Paschal
166   *bottom,* Celebrity Photo/John Paschal
171   *top,* JPI/John Paschal
171   *middle right,* JPI/John Paschal
171   *middle left,* JPI/John Paschal
171   *bottom,* JPI/Aaron Montgomery
175   NBC/Gary Null
176   *left,* JPI/John Paschal
176   *right,* JPI/Aaron Montgomery
177   JPI/John Paschal
178   JPI/John Paschal
179   *left,* JPI/John Paschal
179   *right,* JPI/John Paschal
181   JPI/John Paschal
182   Celebrity Photo/John Paschal
183   Celebrity Photo/John Paschal
185   *top,* JPI/John Paschal
185   *bottom,* JPI/John Paschal
188   Hutchins Photo Agency
193   *top,* NBC
193   *bottom,* JPI/John Paschal
194   JPI/John Paschal
195   Celebrity Photo/John Paschal
196   *top left,* Celebrity Photo/John Paschal
196   *bottom left,* Celebrity Photo/John Paschal
196   *bottom right,* JPI/John Paschal
197   JPI/John Paschal
199   *left,* Hutchins Photo Agency
199   *right,* Hutchins Photo Agency
201   Celebrity Photo/John Paschal
202   *top,* JPI/John Paschal
202   *right,* JPI/John Paschal
205   JPI/John Paschal
207   NBC/Gary Null
209   Celebrity Photo/John Paschal
215   JPI/John Paschal
217   NBC/Alice S. Hall
218   JPI/John Paschal
220   Corday Productions/Jeff Kotz

Map of Salem
4–5   Chip Dox

Floor Plans
Jennifer Buerklander

Drawings of Exterior Homes
John Wiley